EMMANUEL NUHU KURE

PRACTICAL
Prophetic
PRAYER
and Warfare

Pulling Down Strongholds

Behold, the Lord God will come with strong hand,
His arm shall rule for Him . . .

ISAIAH 40:10

PRACTICAL PROPHETIC PRAYER AND WARFARE
PULLING DOWN STRONGHOLDS

Behold, the Lord God
will come with strong hand,
His arm shall rule for Him. . .
Isaiah 40:10

Pastor Emmanuel Nuhu Kure

PRACTICAL PROPHETIC PRAYER AND WARFARE

©2020 by Dr. Emmanuel Nuhu Kure   **First Edition** 1999
ISBN: 978-1-952025-11-2   **Second Edition** 2020

Published by Carpenter's Son Publishing, Franklin, TN
Published in association with Larry Carpenter of Christian Book Services, LLC   **www.christianbookservices.com**

Scriptures are taken from the KING JAMES VERSION (KJV): KING JAMES VERSION, public domain.

Edited by Dr. William Combs
Cover Design by Suzanne Lawing
Interior Design by Dr. William Combs

Forward all inquiries to:
Throneroom (Trust) Ministry, Inc.
Zion International Prayer and Retreat Camp
Throneroom Close, Off Hospital Road
PO Box 266, Kafanchan, Kaduna State, Nigeria.
Tel. Nigeria: +234-8051817164 / US: +1-850-559-0024

Printed in the United States of America

CONTENTS

DEDICATION

Dedicated to the Millennial and Rapture Church. Let us arise and meet the King in victory and great glory, bringing in the sheaves. Also, to the elders around me who have kept faith with God and have established a memorial in heaven in their latter days - Dr. E. Soladoye, Major General [Rtd.] Y. Y. Kure and Dr. Samuel D. Gani. May their remembrance be forever. Let the good fight of faith continue.

ACKNOWLEDGEMENTS

I want to thank all those who contributed to make the publication of this book a success.

Special thanks go to God's faithful saints, namely, Pastor Joseph Kyari, Pastor Naomi David Aruwa for laying down their lives on the altar to ensure the designing and editing of the first edition; and Pastor Gaius Gbowol Dawang and Sister Priscilla Sammani Bawa who also type the manuscript of the first edition. My thanks also go particularly to Pastor William Combs who took it upon himself to see that the second edition is published. Thanks to Larry Carpenter for publishing this edition in the United States.

When the Malachi 3:10 records are written, it shall be recorded that, by your sacrifices, the Church received life.

God bless you.
Kure

INTRODUCTION

The twentieth century Church was characterized by vicissitudes of spiritual encounter from the Azusa Street Revival to the widespread Holy Ghost baptism all over the globe. The Church was, indeed, empowered from on high to do great exploits and domesticate her environment. But, alas, this glorious manifestation of God's glory was beclouded by quests for materialism, careless living and bitter strife, which opened doors for an invasion from hell.

Hell was let loose against the Church and the Church became greatly plagued with all kinds of diseases, infirmaries and barrenness. Thus, the Church became impotent. Hitherto, the Church had been suffering constant defeats from the devil and his cohorts, and creations have been groaning for the earnest manifestation of the sons of God.

As the new millennium is here, the Church cannot afford to remain in abject ignorance and continue to suffer humiliating defeats. Zion must awake and put on her strength.

"AWAKE, awake; put on thy strength, O Zion; put on thy beautiful garments, O Jerusalem, the holy city: for henceforth there shall no more come into thee the uncircumcised and the unclean. Shake thyself from the dust; arise, and sit down, O Jerusalem: loose thyself from the bands of thy neck, O captive daughter of Zion." (Isaiah 52:1-2)

Most believers have become so familiar with spiritual battles that they sometimes carelessly take things for granted, not realizing the implication of what they do. Any time a situation comes against you as a believer, do not hastily say, "By the blood of Jesus, I rebuke you. In Jesus' name, I cast out" etc. This is not the right approach to spiritual warfare. It may eventually not achieve the desired victory.

There are 3 basic steps we need to take to obtain victory, and these are explained below.

STEP 1 - SET UP A STANDARD
STEP 2 - PREPARE THE NATIONS AGAINST HER
STEP 3 - CALL THE KINGDOM OF ARARAT

STEP 1 - SET UP A STANDARD:
The first step in spiritual warfare is to set up a standard and declare the basis of the relationship by which you are springing up to fight. You cannot win any battle until you set the standard. This is the surest way to destroy satanic rights. In Jeremiah 51:27, the Bible says:
"Set ye up a standard in the land, blow the trumpet among the nations, prepare the nations against her, call together against her the kingdoms of Ararat, Minni, and Ashchenaz; appoint a captain against her; cause the horses to come up as the rough caterpillers."

When David came against Goliath, he declared the basis for the warfare by saying:
"Then said David to the Philistine, Thou comest to me with a sword, and with a spear, and with a shield: but I come to thee in the name of the LORD of hosts, the God of the armies of Israel, whom thou hast defied." (1 Samuel 17:45)

Daniel's standard was the Lord of hosts. When a problem comes against you, declare to it that, "It is not by power, nor by might, but I come against you by the blood of Jesus." This means you have withdrawn from the scene and someone mightier has taken over. However, when you rise beyond yourself, like Samson did, you will lose the battle.

In Acts 3, when Peter and John were about to go into the temple, which gate is called Beautiful, they were confronted with a situation of a man crippled from birth who wanted alms. Peter declared his terms of battle by saying, *"Silver and gold have I none; but such as I have I give thee:"* The Bible recorded that as soon as Peter held the crippled man by the right hand and lifted him up, his feet and ankle bones immediately received strength. And he, leaping up, stood and walked.

However, when like Samson, you suddenly rise in every battle and say, "By the blood of Jesus! I come against you in the name of Jesus!" you will fight for a long time. That does not mean that the efficacy of the blood of Jesus is not real. It means you are quick in drawing the sword as though it were in your power to launch out. That was Samson's approach, not the Lord's. Hence Samson failed. Presumptuousness does not produce results in spiritual battles.

The Lord's Prayer, which Jesus taught His disciples to start by saying, *"Our Father which art in heaven, Hallowed be thy name. Thy kingdom come. Thy will be done in earth..."* typifies His approach to things pertaining to life and godliness. So, we must understand that everything starts with God, His Kingdom and authority, not yours.

Set up the standard. Jesus is the standard. Some of us take glory for the battles won in the name of Jesus. We are fond of saying, "I delivered the man of demons."

STEP 2 - PREPARE THE NATIONS AGAINST HER
The Bible says in Jeremiah 51:28, *"Prepare against her the nations."* When you call them (your adversaries) by their names,

tell them to relate by their captains and the earth shall tremble, for every purpose of the Lord shall be performed. Henceforth, every purpose and every word of God shall be performed in your life and against those that gather against you. Isaiah says they shall surely gather. But they shall fall for your sake. Amen.

STEP 3 - CALL THE KINGDOM OF ARARAT:
Call the kingdom of Ararat. This represents the forces that are against you. Therefore, summon the horses and the caterpillars against them. Who are the horses? They are the armies of vengeance, the battalions that fight wars. The commander of the hosts of heaven will release them to come to your aid with their swords for vengeance. God says, *"Vengeance is mine; I will repay, saith the Lord."*

Beware of stepping into witchcraft by taking the teaching of this book out of scriptural balance and delve into the extreme - by using oil, dust, ashes, etc. - excessively for everything, more from fear and insecurity than from obedience and the leading of the Holy Spirit. This approach does not follow the patterns set in the Scripture. Romans 8:14 says, *"For as many as are led by the Spirit of God, they are the sons of God."* However, when you use them based on the revelation you have from constantly fellowshipping with God, they produce glaring and irrefutable results.

This biblical pattern should flow naturally in your prayers and Bible study life with God at the center of the matter. At this juncture, it is imperative to emphasize that if you only operate at this level of strategic spiritual warfare when you are confronted with the problems of life, it is an indication that you have turned it into a mere religious ritual and witchcraft, and this is not acceptable in heaven. You must make the patterns taught in this book a part of your normal daily life with God,

not an antidote to apply only when you are in trouble. Thereafter, a permanent shield of fellowship will be established for
you in heaven.

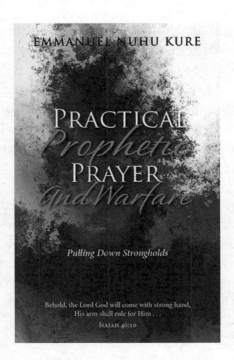

CHAPTER 1

SPIRITUAL PROVISIONS IN HEAVENLY PLACES

THERE IS A company of innumerable angels in heaven who specialize in different assignments. They are ministering spirits that are always at the service of believers who live and walk by the spirit. When you have a soul-tie with heaven, as a child of God, your soul is hidden in Christ Jesus in heavenly places above all principalities and the powers of darkness. You can call heaven to open up to you and these angels will always be ready to carry out assignments on your behalf.

One of the reasons why the Church has not benefited much from the services of these angels is that most of us have not learnt to walk and live by the Spirit. Notice that the Bible says in Hebrews 1:14, *"Are they not all ministering spirits, sent forth to minister for them who shall be heirs of salvation?"* They are spirits, not flesh and blood like we are. Therefore we must work and live by the spirit before they can be useful to us.

Do you know that there are professionals in heaven just as there are on earth? In heaven there are architects, building engineers, estate engineers, etc., all of whose work is to design, construct and maintain respectively. So also are there professionals who specialize in warfare. None operates outside their field. They walk in their columns and maintain order. They don't break ranks.

Do you know that there are spirit beings whose daily routine is to work for you? They go to the office with you, move about with you, always staying by your side to guide and protect you against whatever comes your way. You must learn to engage them. Otherwise, they will be on holiday perpetually. They work only when they are instructed. Please don't render these angels redundant.

It is unfortunate and pathetic that while the earth is full of pressures, the resources of heaven are being underutilized. This means that most of the pressures you go through are unnecessary if you learn to tap into these resources. Jesus says: *"Take my yoke upon you, and learn of me; for I am meek and lowly in heart: and ye shall find rest unto your souls. For my yoke is easy, and my burden is light."* (Matthew 11:29-30)

Have you realized that there are baby sitters in heaven who are meant to take care of your babies? How many times have you called God to use angels to form a shield around your baby who is about to die? Until you call them, they will not come. When you fail to call them, your suffering becomes self-inflicted, because it means you have failed to utilize the provisions from heaven. The Bible says in Romans 8:6 that *"For to be carnally minded is death; but to be spiritually minded is life and peace."* To walk in the reality and benefit of what I am teaching in this book you must have a spiritual mindset as instructed by the scripture.

THE RAVENOUS BIRD
When a bird is said to be ravenous, it means it feeds on flesh, like a vulture. Having prepared for battle by setting up a standard, begin to call forth the professionals in heaven that the Bible refers to as ravenous birds from the nest.

"Calling a ravenous bird from the east, the man that executeth my counsel from a far country: yea, I have spoken it, I will also bring it to pass; I have purposed it, I will also do it." (Isaiah 46:11)

Birds are occasionally associated with witches and wizards, women in cults and water spirit fraternities. They are used as symbols of power and authority. Sometimes birds are sent to torment people's lives through witchcraft. When a bird is sent to disturb you in the night or day, arise and send the ravenous bird to drive it away. Release the Spirit of God against the spirits that wage war against you. If they are invisible to your spirit, they cannot be invisible to the all-seeing eyes of God Who sees the end from the beginning. So, if you discern an evil bird crying on a tree near your house, open your windows, send a ravenous bird against it and pray in this manner, *"Father, the oppressions that came with this evil bird must go. I call upon you to release a ravenous bird to drive it away."* The bird must obey the word of the Lord.

May I ask you: Is there anything eating up your life everyday so you feel like your whole life is depreciating? The way out of this battle is to call the ravenous bird. You must go deeper in spiritual battle. Pray by saying,

"Father, the day has come for warfare. Where are the warriors in heaven? Let them answer me now. Where is the God of covenant? In the name of Jesus my God, solve this problem for me now. Oh problem, I have nothing against you but I come against you in the name of my Lord Jesus Christ by whose authority I have dominion over you."

By this prayer, you have set the standard from where the battle will be decided. You are not the one fighting. Revelations 3 says, *"I know thy works: behold, I have set before thee an open door, and no man can shut it: for thou hast a little strength, and hast kept my word, and hast not denied my name."* This means that there is power in the little strength the Lord has given you to destroy your enemy. Set up a standard and begin to call heavenly provisions to help you.

Are you growing lean every day without any overt cause? Maybe someone has told you that somebody is sucking your blood. Do you have a child that keeps growing leaner, in spite of good feeding and adequate medical care? Has a medical examination shown that he had worms - yet even after treatment he still continues to lose weight?

Tell God that you and your child shall not die but live to declare His glory:

"Oh you that eat my flesh, I will not die. Not by power nor by might, but by the Spirit of God. Who are you, oh great mountain that is destroying me? It is by grace that I exist. I come against you in Jesus' name. My God, release the ravenous bird against whichever bird is eating up my flesh, in Jesus' name,

Amen."

THE FISHERS AND THE HUNTERS
If you do not know the cause of your suffering, tell God to release the hunters, according to Jeremiah 16:16:

"Behold, I will send for many fishers, saith the LORD, and they shall fish them; and after will I send for many hunters, and they shall hunt them from every mountain, and from every hill, and out of the holes of the rocks."

The hunters and fishers are sent against forces of darkness like witches and wizards whose bases of operation are caves, mountains, rivers and riversides.

If you have an ailment, the cause of which you do not understand, tell God to release the hunters to find out what the cause of your ailment is and destroy it. Perhaps the engine of your car has knocked consecutively after each repair, or you wake up in the morning and discovered you are confused for no visible reason, so much so that you head begins to spin. Tell God to release the heavenly hunters and fishers to unravel the mystery behind each case.

Are you a businessman whose business is nose-diving without any obvious reason? It is time for your enemies to be on the run so that you can have peace of mind. If you are a promising civil servant but things tend to go wrong with your office because somebody is planning evil against you. Go to the office and say, *"God, I do not understand what is happening to me. My God, release the fishers to discover the reason for my suffering in Jesus' name."*

Have you not read in Ezekiel 5 that ordinary men will set a trap and fall into it? You too, can set a trap for them and they will fall into it. Just release the fishers and hunters to set their nets and traps against your enemies. There is no spell that has no counter force in heaven. It is lack of knowledge that makes many Christians languish in calamities. Search the Scripture that speaks about Jesus and the power of His resurrection.

A sister in Kano suddenly took ill. She was a wonderful Deeper Life Church member, a leader and a perfect example of God's finger. She would preach, heal the sick and cast out demons. A certain mysterious sickness came upon her with excruciating pain that sent her fainting. On one occasion, she went into a coma. When she was rushed to the hospital, on seeing her, the Indian doctor shouted, "Take her away from me! Take her away from me immediately!" Even though doctors are always eager to receive patients, this doctor saw an evil spirit in this case, so he ran for his dear life.

The saints who took her to the hospital had no other choice than to take her back. But where next to take her? They had earlier taken her to a Deeper Life Church in Kano where she had been prayed for throughout the night. In the midst of this confusion, the sister woke up and said," Take me to Kure, he knows what is happening. If you don't take me to him, I will die."

When I saw her lying down, I called her name repeatedly, but there was no response. After she regained consciousness, she said, "Don't let me die." I asked her what had gone wrong. She said she didn't know but some people said she had a demon. But since I knew how transparent her life was, I could bail her out of her dying state. "Don't let me die," she repeated, and went back into a coma. Tears came out of my eyes and I began to pray. I pleaded with the Lord not to let a saint suffer such a painful agony. I wept bitterly because each time she came around, she wriggled in severe pain.

I was bewildered. All the time, I asked God what to do and He told me that the next time she came to, I should hold her hands and look straight into her eyes the way Peter did to the cripple at the Beautiful Gate and tell her to transfer all she had to me. I obeyed the Lord. God said if she did that, she would not faint and neither would she die. When she looked into my eyes with her hands around my body, she received new inspiration and strength.

After this, I again asked God what's to do next. Her said I should call out from her life the issues that were destroying her. It took an intense concentration on my part to know exactly what the Lord's will was concerning her situation. The Holy Spirit was dictating the battle.

As I began to call forth the issues as directed by the Lord, many things began to happen. Interestingly enough., when I mentioned Bonny River, the sister screamed. I asked her if she had a covenant in her life. She said she could recall that, as a little child, a certain woman took her to the shores of Bonny River to perform a sacrifice. The woman asked her to undress and she remained naked while the ritual was being performed. She now remembered that something which represented her seed, came out of her after some incantation. This revelation gave me a clue to the core of the problem. I now realized that her womb had been removed during the course of the sacrifice. In fact, she confirmed that, prior to this time, a doctor had examined her and discovered that she had no womb - it had been removed. Meanwhile, demons had begun to kill her when the myth story was being unraveled. The core of the matter was about to be revealed.

The Lord further told me that a frog had swallowed her womb and the frog was still alive in the belly of a fish. However, when I was about to speak to the river, the Lord restrained me and told me rather to call forth the provisions in heaven to bind the strong man that controlled the frog and the fish - Olumba. The strong man had many thrones scattered in many rivers, one of which was the Bonny River. I heard the Spirit of the Lord say, "I give you the freedom to begin to learn about provisions in heaven and discover more through diligent, personal Bible study."

When God told me to settle the battle array in heaven, I asked, "Where are the men of war? Let them come out of their different formations and stand right on top of Bonny River." Thus, I set the battle at Bonny River. Having done that, I asked the Lord what the next step was. He told me to release the fishers and the hunters.

What came out was not the palace but a huge man dressed in a flowing white gown. Both the sister and I simultaneously shouted, "Olumba!" I was gripped by fear because I had never encountered such warfare. She began to scream and pull her hands having seen the mystery of the man that was killing her. God warned me not to panic lest both of us should die.

The man stood there, huge and fierce and charging against us. God told me to send the chains. I called forth angels that rule principalities and powers, and commanded them to bind the man. Then I saw the chains flying. As soon as Thelma was bound, he started screaming and roaring.

Again, the Lord told me not to go into battle with the man but to command the spirit of the man so that he would never rule over the lady's life again. The Lord further said I should release the fishers to Fish out the fish and any being that hitherto held the sister bound. I commanded the fish to vomit the frog, which in turn would vomit the womb.

The sister's hands let go of my body. She began to scream

speaking in tongues and breathing heavily. Her deliverance had taken place. I now went closer to the lady and began to command healing into her as instructed by the Holy Spirit. Praise God, the sister was delivered and she has never had cause to faint or suffer such horrible attacks again.

THE FLYING ROLL

In Zechariah 5:1, 3-4, the Bible says there is a spirit in heaven called the "Flying Roll," whose function is to catch thieves wherever they may be.

"THEN I turned, and lifted up mine eyes, and looked, and behold a flying roll. Then said he unto me, This is the curse that goeth forth over the face of the whole earth: for every one that stealeth shall be cut off as on this side according to it; and every one that sweareth shall be cut off as on that side according to it. I will bring it forth, saith the LORD of hosts, and it shall enter into the house of the thief, and into the house of him that sweareth falsely by my name: and it shall remain in the midst of his house, and shall consume it with the timber thereof and the stones thereof."

Do not send this spirit to fight witches and wizards. It has two targets: thieves and those who swear falsely.

If anyone accuses you falsely, call the flying roll and he will defend you because you are innocent. You do not even have to go to your closet before praying. However, do not call the flying roll when you are guilty.

Only herbalists or witch doctors would fight for a guilty person. If you are born again and you swear falsely, you will be in trouble. Things will begin to go wrong with your life. If you start a business by cheating your partners, you will lose in the end.

If you are accused falsely in your place of work, tell your boss, "Sir, if I were guilty, I would admit it. However, I dare to say that, by the Lord God of heaven, I am innocent." Then, turn to your accusers and say, "You are accusing me. I call the spirit of the flying roll to judge between you and me." I assure you that even if you are sacked, you will be reinstated by the time the spirit has accomplished the task. They will not only beg you to come back, but will promote you and thereafter regard you with awe.

During one of the annual anniversary programs organized by the Full Gospel Business Men's Fellowship International, Zaria chapter, a man's car was stolen. Unfortunately, that was the first time he was attending any program where I was the speaker, perhaps after much persuasion from his wife. During the program, I saw him raise his hand slightly above his head to give his life to Jesus Christ. However, he came out at the end of the program only to discover that his car had been stolen, leaving him with the keys in his hands.

When the matter was reported to me, I sent for the man. I could read from his face that he was already regretting attending the meeting. He perhaps was blaming his wife for persuading him to attend the program. The excitement of being born again was over and the joy of salvation stolen in an instant.

I took the keys in my hands and prayed that the flying roll be released from heaven to catch the thief. "Father, let the thief be pursued with the urgency this case deserves while the battle is still hot. According to your word in Zechariah 5, let the flying roll catch the thief. Your word cannot lie. On earth, stop the car and let it be abandoned or have the tire punctured or be returned to the man's house in Jesus' name." The next morning, the car was found parked by the man's house.

It is time to begin calling the spiritual provisions in heaven.

Call them by name. When you waste time speaking in tongues, they will wait for you to finish but will act only when you give the appropriate command when you speak.

In Zechariah 5:4, the Bible says the Lord Himself will release the flying roll unto the house of the thief. He will supervise the work of the flying roll until the thief is completely dealt with. He and his entire family will be routed out.

I had cause to pray for a prominent paramount ruler in Port Harcourt, River State, Nigeria, concerting someone who had owed him thousands of Naira for years. He said he wanted the man to repay the debt unfailingly that year. I told the chief it would take God to do that and that the flying roll was capable of forcing the man to pay the money. After the first time we prayed, the man contacted the chief and promised to pay the debt that year.

Nevertheless, when next we met with the chief and I discovered that the man had not fulfilled the promise, I assured the chief that the matter would definitely be resolved in his favor. I told him about the mystery of the flying roll which could catch as well as judge any thief. The chief said he would not mind if God chose not to punish the thief provided the man refunded the money. We prayed and sent the flying roll into the situation. Thanks be to God that chief's debt was paid.

This man is in his sixties and in the Full Gospel Business Men's Fellowship. He knew the mystery of the flying roll. When the spirit comes, he will ravage the man out of his household without leaving any remnant.

Who said the most dangerous being is Satan? There are other beings in heaven more dangerous than Satan. All your enemies who threaten to kill you are ignorant of that. Once you release the right spirit, the devourers in your life will disappear.

THE CARPENTERS

In Zechariah 1:18-19, 21, the Bible says that there are carpenters in heaven who have the anointing to beat the forces of darkness with hammers. These evil forces are spiritual horns that stand against you.

"Then lifted I up mine eyes, and saw, and behold four horns. And I said unto the angel that talked with me, What be these? And he answered me, These are the horns which have scattered Judah, Israel, and Jerusalem. Then said I, What come these to do? And he spake, saying, These are the horns which have scattered Judah, so that no man did lift up his head: but these are come to fray them, to cast out the horns of the Gentiles, which lifted up their horn over the land of Judah to scatter it."

If you have worked for many years without anyone recognizing you labor, it's time to arise and shine for the glory of the Lord is risen upon you. Release the carpenters against any person attempting to stop you from attaining the full potentials the Lord endowed you with before He formed you in your mother's womb.

THE DESTROYING ANGELS

In Psalms 78:49, the Bible talks of destroying angels whose assignment is to make trouble, to being indignation and the wrath of God.

"He cast upon them the fierceness of his anger, wrath, and indignation, and trouble, by sending evil angels among them."

If anybody wants to cause trouble for you in order to cause your downfall, call the evil angels to keep them busy. You will discover thereafter that you are free from every form of bondage and from any person's scheme to destroy you.

The Bible says the "Egyptians" that have been kept hitherto bound will come under God's wrath. *"He spared not their soul from death but gave their life over to the pestilence."* Yes, for you His people, the Lord will tend up to the border of His sanctuary, even to the morning which His right hand has purchased.

THE WASTER
In Isaiah 54:15-16, the Bible talks about the waster whose work is to destroy. The Holy Spirit releases him whenever the situation demand urgent intervention.

"Behold, they shall surely gather together, but not by me: whosoever shall gather together against thee shall fall for thy sake."

There must be a groaning before the waster is sent. Otherwise, some people will abuse the provision and consequently destroy God's purpose in heaven and on earth. The scriptural reference above is an eye opener. Our enemies will certainly rise against us. But God readily has counter spirits to destroy and completely liquidate the enemies and their controls. Let it neither be mentioned that the devil poured ashes on you and, as a result, the struggles of life overtook and destroyed you, nor ever be said that you were helpless in the days of battle.

You can now see why we cry the cry of Moses, *"Let God arise and His enemies be scattered."* Jesus is seated at the right hand of God making intercession for the saints. He is the Rock that is higher than us. So call upon heaven to send the right help in times of need.

The day and the hour to purge the heavens is come. We shall not spare any demon as we call upon the sacrifice of the blood of Jesus that stands and speaks for us in heaven before the throne of God. When the blood of Jesus Christ calls from heaven, the earth will begin to vomit everything, every mystery that is hidden against us. Let every provision of heaven be released to show forth God's glory. Come Holy Spirit and let the thrones in heaven spread before us. Let every host of glory spread before us. Let every conspiracy of hell be spoiled in the name of Jesus. Amen!

THE SERPENT

"I SAW the Lord standing upon the altar: and he said, Smite the lintel of the door, that the posts may shake: and cut them in the head, all of them; and I will slay the last of them with the sword: he that fleeth of them shall not flee away, and he that escapeth of them shall not be delivered. Though they dig into hell, thence shall mine hand take them; though they climb up to heaven, thence will I bring them down: And though they hide themselves in the top of Carmel, I will search and take them out thence; and though they be hid from my sight in the bottom of the sea, thence will I command the serpent, and he shall bite them: And though they go into captivity before their enemies, thence will I command the sword, and it shall slay them: and I will set mine eyes upon them for evil, and not for good." (Amos 9:1-4)

One of the greatest mysteries of our time will be the revelation of the spirit called leviathan. He is risen already over the nations to threaten, subject and bring death upon them.

The Lord has opened our eyes to see the mystery coming upon the earth: little serpents have been released to bite and slaughter a lot of people so much that close to half the world's population may experience death by the close of 2000 AD. Some will die by strange diseases and illnesses that defy treatment. The serpents will release their venoms on earth by the powers of darkness, preparatory to the reign of the antichrist. The tail of the dragon controlled by the leviathan spirit will control more than a third of the earth, leaving the earth desperate for false miracles as a solution to the antichrist that will eventually pave the way for his reign. This is meant to ensure a terror of death - to hunt people and nations these last three years - 1998 - 2000 AD - as it has never been before. No clan or family will be spared. Christians and non-Christians alike will be affected directly or indirectly - either through relations or friends.

A scriptural study of leviathan and the dragon will help you understand the full implications of the above situation in individuals and nations. In fact, the spirit of leviathan the dragon is risen to inflict great pains on nations in order to affect and influence governments to create a conducive environment for antichrist activities in the nations and a doomsday for the Church and her testimony. The watchmen and all they that seek the Lord out of a pure heart must necessarily take their place before God and answer back.

It is leviathan that leads and spurs the ancient spirits to war; he has awakened and released the spirit of death over the nations and their tribes. This explains why there is a great pull to shed blood all over the nations. Ancient spirits are hovering over the nations. The standards raised against leviathan are two: the blood of Jesus and the confessions and the clinging to the word of God by the Church. The sword which happens to be an instrument of divine judgement against marine or water spirits or river covenants found in Amos 9:3:

"And though they hide themselves in the top of Carmel, I will search and take them out thence; and though they be hid from my sight in the bottom of the sea, thence will I command the serpent, and he shall bite them:"

The Lord calls it "MY SERPENT." It is the covenant spirit of God in the form of a serpent that searches out the hiddenmysteries of Satan against us from the sea. Ask God for it, groan in your prayer through to the throne of grace, call for it to be released. Declare it against the marine powers of the sea and their influence around you in the physical, be it in the office, family, business, relationships, fellowship, church, etc., and against your nation and government. Then the Lord shall, through the mystery of the snake, devour - "bite." The Lord said:

"I have long time holden my peace; I have been still, and refrained myself: now will I cry like a travailing woman; I will destroy and devour at once." (Isaiah 42:14)

The serpent from the throne of God is one of the spirits God uses to destroy and devour. It is one of the solutions to those biting demons and spirits of sudden death through strange illnesses and diseases. Neutralize their poisons by the blood of Jesus, attack and cut them off (devour them) by the serpent of the Most High God. My friend and fellow pilgrim, arise to war for your sake and for the sake of your nation, for this is the only remnant, so that testimony can remain for your God and for Zion, and your portion secured.

Tradition is threatening everywhere. It is already swallowing up the faith of many so-called Christians. Nations are restless. This is one battle the Church cannot afford to lose. It will either win this battle or risk losing the nations to another dark age. These ancient spirits, propelled by leviathan, are pushing the nations to catastrophe, confusing everything - from economy to politics, through commerce, health, to social life, etc. Even the Church is not spared the onslaught of this ancient spirit that has eroded set standards in the society.

WHO CAN BRING DOWN FIRE AND SOLUTIONS?
It is as Hezekiah described it: *a day of trouble and rebukes and blasphemy."* (2 Kings 18:28, 19:1-28) The same ancient spirit that rose against Hezekiah is risen now. Only three categories of people will qualify to ascend the throne of grace to bring

down fire and solutions. They are:

1. The "Virgin Daughters of Zion" (2 Kings 19:21): These are the holy men and women (holy Church) who have kept the path of truth of the Holy Scripture and have kept their garments unspotted. They shall bring down the fire of God upon these spirits.

"THEN I looked, and, behold, in the firmament that was above the head of the cherubims there appeared over them as it were a sapphire stone, as the appearance of the likeness of a throne. And he spake unto the man clothed with linen, and said, Go in between the wheels, even under the cherub, and fill thine hand with coals of fire from between the cherubims, and scatter them over the city. And he went in in my sight. Now the cherubims stood on the right side of the house, when the man went in; and the cloud filled the inner court." (Ezekiel 10:1-3)

2. Elders: Those from fifty and above whose mouths have not been given to guile. They shall declare liberty upon the land.

"And ye shall hallow the fiftieth year, and proclaim liberty throughout all the land unto all the inhabitants thereof: it shall be a jubilee unto you; and ye shall return every man unto his possession, and ye shall return every man unto his family." (Leviticus 25:10)

"And round about the throne were four and twenty seats: and upon the seats I saw four and twenty elders sitting, clothed in white raiment; and they had on their heads crowns of gold." (Revelation 4:4)

3. Covenant Prophetic Praying Women: These are women who have the mantle to play a significant role in the battles of this last hour. There are spiritual secrets about the holy, faithful and zealous woman many of which have not come alive.

They bear the sacred oils that hold the solutions to this last hour (Jeremiah 10:17-24, 31:22-23).

The last two must meet the conditions of the first to qualify. These three categories of people qualify to call forth these mysteries of God's spiritual provisions. For this is the hour that the Lord has revealed in this book. If you are not born again or you are not living right, it is time to cast out the works of darkness in your life so that's you may be grafted into God's olive tree and begin to appropriate God's provisions.

"For if thou wert cut out of the olive tree which is wild by nature, and wert graffed contrary to nature into a good olive tree: how much more shall these, which be the natural branches, be graffed into their own olive tree?" (Romans 11:24).

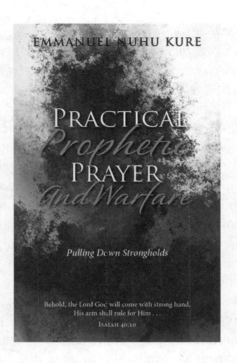

CHAPTER 2

BURNING THE ALTARS OF DARKNESS

"So mightily grew the word of God
AND PREVAILED"

THE **WORD OF GOD** exploded, grew mightily and prevailed when the instrument used by hell in battle were burnt.

"Many of them also which used CURIOUS ARTS brought their BOOKS together, and BURNED them before all men: and they counted the price of them, and found it fifty thousand pieces of silver" (Acts 19:19).

You must go on a violent spiritual and physical rampage before your bounds can finally be broken and your release established. Even as these spirits of God's judgment and divine manifestation act on your behalf to avert a reoccurrence of battle, you must set out on a spiritual war-path to destroy the instruments of war which your enemies use against you. The Bible says they were burnt. So, burn them in the Spirit as you confront them in prayers. Release the consuming fire of God on them.

The Lord says He knows where they live. So let His Spirit guide your spiritual missiles of fire and judgment. The instrument of judgment you must use against their mediums and instruments of war must be fire.

The Bible says, *"...Whom the Lord shall consume with the spirit of his mouth, and shall destroy with the brightness of his coming"* (2 Thess. 2:8). Revelations 4:5 and 5:6 reveal the seven spirits of God that are lamps of fire sent into all the earth to consume Satan and every revelation of his spirits in every part of the world.

We must rise to the challenges of the time, lest we and the testimony of the Lord should be consumed, and the battle of the ages be lost in our generation. We must rise and ask God to arise on our behalf, and His altars will rise with us from heaven.

According to Deuteronomy 32, their treasures and storehouses are where the instruments of Satan's warfare are kept. Amos tells us they are in the constellations amongst the stars and in the astral world. That is why the Bible says we fight them in heavenly places (Ephesians 6) and enjoins us, therefore, to CAST DOWN their imaginations and subject them to Christ.

We must go to those places in prayer and break them up using the fire of the seven spirits of God. We must cast them down and turn them to ashes. Thereafter, we shall call forth in the same breath the new things from heaven that should take their places. The Bible puts it as *"Calling forth those things that be not as though they were"* (Romans 4:17).

Though they were not physically in your warfare, you have called them forth as prepared from the treasures of heaven to take over as answered prayer where Satan has occupied. So, set the treasures and the ammunition on fire. And, as you achieve victory, call forth replacement from the treasures of heaven.

Do not destroy their instruments of war in the spiritual realm, but also bring out all the physical elements and representation in your house or environment and destroy them. Things like carvings that represent gods or demonic cultures or ideas or lustful nudities or labyrinths of confusion and madness should not be spared.

Books on astral travels, transcendental Eastern meditations and religions, cultist formulations, scientific spiritualism of any kind (Christian or not), new abstracts, etc., should be burnt to ashes.

Such items form parts of the bond of covenant or altars (though in book form or carvings) for the spirits that rule the physical territory (area or district) where you live.

It is one of the means through which spirits project themselves into your environment. Their mere presence in your house alone conjures astral spirits and focuses their attention on your home affairs whether you believe in them or not, or whether you practice their teachings or not, or whether they are there only for intellectual or decorative reasons or not. The letters in those books will pull into your home the forces in the atmosphere.

Their presence might be responsible for the gloom and stagnancy being experience in some homes. Please, dear reader, if you have such books or know someone who has them in his or her house, I advise you to prayerfully burn them. When you have done this, the spirits of bondage attracted by those books will leave the environment, and the atmosphere around you will change for the better.

If you cannot do this by yourself, take them to a pastor of a Bible-believing church whom you trust. When you burn them, the spirits and the life in those writings or carvings or symbols are released to go back to where they came from. You will notice that when Manoah, Sampson's father, burnt the sacrifices unto God, the angel used it as a doorway or an avenue to go back to God.

"So Manoah took a kid with a meat offering, and offered it upon a rock unto the LORD: and the angel did wondrously; and Manoah and his wife looked on. For it came to pass, when the flame went up toward heaven from off the altar, that the angel of the LORD ascended in the flame of the altar..." (Judges 13:19-20).

You release spirits by fire. You let them loose up to their root. There is no other way to do this. No matter how expensive those pictures, books, clothes or instruments may be. The items burnt in Acts 19:19 were worth fifty thousand pieces of silver. Yet they were burnt, not sold or given out or thrown away, but burnt. That is the only way to break whatever is caging your miracles. Burn them, both in the heavenly places and in your physical environment, as Gideon did in his father's house, and your yoke will break for the word (your miracle) to come true and prevail.

"And it came to pass the same night, that the Lord said unto him, Take thy father's young bullock, even the second bullock of seven years old, and throw down the altar of Baal that thy father hath, and cut down the grove that is by it" (Judges 6:25).

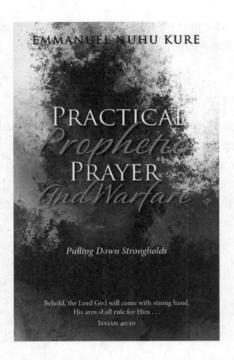

CHAPTER
3

SPIRITUAL GATES
AND DOORWAYS

WHEN WE TALK about gates, we are not making reference to ordinary doorways. Rather, we are talking about the mystery of existence of our environment channels through which things happen in our natural world, the channels the devil uses to afflict us. They can best be described as gates or doorways because they are the words the Bible has employed to help us understand how these things operate. Spiritual gates are also channels through which we receive divine favor and divine blessings.

THE CAULDRON

The word "cauldron" is a phenomenon of witches and wizards. It is the pot in which satanists cook the lives of men and make sacrifices. Every city has a cauldron in which the witches' council cooks the affairs of that city. There may be different kinds of witches. But when it comes to cooking a city, they never disagree in this matter.

The Lord says He will judge, and His judgment will take place at the border. *"This city shall not be your cauldron .."* was the cry of the prophet. It was a cry from the throne of grace.

"This city shall not be your caldron, neither shall ye be the flesh in the midst thereof; but I will judge you in the border of Israel: And ye shall know that I am the Lord: for ye have not walked in my statutes, neither executed my judgments, but have done after the manners of the heathen that are round about you." (Ezekiel 11:11-12)

Some of those cookings take place on the rocks, some by the riverside, some under the sea and some on land. In fact, some are done in public places. That is why we have to pass through the borders so that, as we pass through them to the city, we will be canceling that which has been set on the city.

Verse 13 of the above scripture says, *"And it came to pass when I prophesied..."* When you prophesy, you will see physical results.

The prophet only went in obedience to the command he received without knowing that what he was doing could kill people. When he prophesied, the Bible says even the cauldron devoured Pelatiah - he died. Until heaven begins to hear a voice prophesying in the right places, we cannot begin to get results - the earth will just not open up.

HOW TO RECOGNISE GATES IN CITIES

As the life of a city is controlled by gates, so also are human lives controlled by gates. Everything has its own gate. If you are able to control spiritual gates in the form of physical symbols, you will gain control over the city and the people in it and destroy the spirits that are transferred to influence your life and environments. You will be able to keep them out of your life. However, until you are ready to begin to pray prophetic prayers, you cannot do this.

Every entry point on the road into a city is a gate. That is why we sometimes see witches and wizards singing and walking barefoot all over the street in the early hours of the morning. They are making contacts with the various gates on the roads, up to the borders of the city. The Brotherhood of the Cross and Star, as well as many spiritualists and the so-called "spiritual churches" do that a lot. Occasionally, some orthodox churches also do it, especially those with questionable doctrines. For witches and wizards, it is their consuming passion to take over the gates and control the people in the city.

Whether you like it or not, you have to get involved in the warfare in your city according to the pattern in Ezekiel we just read. Therein lies the mystery of existence.

It should be an eye opener for you that sacrifices are most times placed at T-junctions in the form of food: chicken, eggs, palm oil, old coins or cowries, etc. Intersections are always a point of attraction for sacrifices, both in Nigeria and across the world. They know that such places can represent gates, a spiritual inlet, from where they can use such sacrifices to influence Satan to control the city and its inhabitants.

Trees with deep holes underneath are other points of attraction for sacrifices. These too represent spiritual outlets, spiritual gates. When you see people form a ring around a tree or make a mysterious circle or tie a rope or a piece of cloth around it in a fetish manner, just recognize that place is a gate. It is a power that controls an aspect of that city.

The situation is the same in our village too. Wherever there is a shrine or an altar, it represents a gate. Anywhere you see satanic (juju) priests meeting in your village, it is a gate, a doorway for demonic spirits.

When you drive around your city gates, especially the toll gate areas and any other place the Spirit of God shows you, you can stop there for a while, anoint the place and say, *"Lift up your heads, O Ye gates, and let the King of Glory come in."* By that act, you destroy satanic altars there and establish God's own altar. From then on, things are bound to begin to change for the better in that locality.

In Genesis, the Bible records a sample of an altar built by Jacob:

"And Jacob awaked out of his sleep, and he said, Surely the LORD is in this place; and I knew it not... And Jacob rose up early in the morning, and took the stone that he had put for his pillows, and set it up for a pillar, and poured oil upon the top of it." (Genesis 28:16, 18)

By setting up that stone and pouring oil on it, Jacob had built an altar unto the Lord. Shrines are used in the demonic world to symbolize a gate. A lot of care goes into choosing the site for a shrine. If there were no demons relating with that place, they would not put a shrine there. Therefore, wherever you see a shrine, know that the gate of the power of darkness is there. Thus, every shrine represents a gate.

That is why Gideon, in Judges 6, had to pull down the altar from his father's house. He was destroying the gate in his house. This is why you must begin to address the shrine in your family's house, clan and village, if there is any. Otherwise, hell will continue to rule there and, indeed, confuse your community.

In Isaiah 28:5-6, the Bible says it shall be strength to those who turn the battle to the gate:

"In that day shall the LORD of hosts be for a crown of glory, and for a diadem of beauty, unto the residue of his people, And for a spirit of judgment to him that sitteth in judgment, and for strength to them that turn the battle to the gate."

When you raise a cry, speak against the gates of the grave, the gates of death. When you speak in a land and pray against the principalities that rule that land, please address the gates from where they rule, the inlet by which they enter into that land.

No demon operates in a land without coming through a gate. Without gates or altars, demons cannot come in. Altars sustain and keep them. Each time you see people building physical altars, they are building a doorway for Satan.

In fact, many religious organizations are building special altars now. If you belong to one of these groups, get out of it! Some of them use candles, some use flowers, etc. By so doing, they are raising altars where they conjure demons. These altars can only lead to hell. So get out of them fast.

Anywhere libation is poured, a gate is being opened. So, when you pour libation, you are simply opening the secrets of darkness, establishing a gate or conjuring spirits.

There is also the gate of righteousness. This is the one that prolongs the life of a Christian.

I shall not die, but live, and declare the works of the Lord... Open to me the gates of righteousness: I will go into them, and I will praise the LORD: This gate of the LORD, into which the righteous shall enter. (PSALM 118:17, 19-20)

It is the gate of righteousness that ensures our salvation. It is the one that keeps us alive. Therefore, when you confess, "I *shall not die but live...*" also make sure you are fulfilling the other part of righteousness because it is the gate of righteousness that ensures that you live and not die. The Bible says people have to go without the gate to meet Jesus Christ:

"*Wherefore Jesus also, that he might sanctify the people with his own blood, suffered without the gate. Let us go forth therefore unto him without the camp, bearing his reproach.*" (Hebrews 13:12-13)

This means that even Jesus brought salvation outside the gates. The city is controlled from the gates.

There are gates in the air, on land, on the seas and under the seas. There are gates also by the seashore. When you see people pouring libation or making sacrifices by the seashore, they are opening doorways for the sea to transfer the demons inside back to them on land. Therefore, when you pour anointing oil and speak God's word, the earth hears and responds. That is why when you anoint a place that has troubled you and command the trouble to stop, the sensitivity in that place is supposed to open up to your prayer. That is where the anointing oil comes in. Nevertheless, please do not abuse it by using it to wash your toes, neck, mouth, eyes, head and other parts of your body. This can lead you into error without you realizing it.

Everything you do, even when it is slightly out of order in the physical, must never be out of order with the Word of God! You must ensure it is a clear message from heaven. If it disagrees with the Word, no matter how convincing you are of what spirit told you to do it, do not do it. The Holy Spirit will never contradict the Word of God.

If, therefore, you are already engaging in excesses in your home, using holy water or holy oil to engage in all kinds extremity, put it through the Word. If it has no biblical basis, stop it today. Otherwise witches and demons will oppress you. Problems that should otherwise be easily solved will become insurmountable. They may provide solutions to your present problem only to replace it with a thousand others. STOP IT NOW!

In breaking gates, anointing oil is very vital. Declare a fast and use anointing oil to break yokes. Send the words and anoint the place. The oil will stamp those words you send there. It will remain there and eat up that place. Olive oil is scriptural, as buttressed in Zechariah 4. The Bible talks about the golden olive trees in heaven. The Scripture uses he words "olive trees" because it reveals that God Himself released golden oil from the olive trees through the golden pipe into the golden bowl that was upon the golden candlestick.

That candlestick was Zerubbabel who was a human being. But he was not just an ordinary citizen but the governor of Judah whom God released to rebuild the waste places. Without the golden oil, the waste places would not have been rebuilt. Oils are used to rebuild waste places -- places that have been plundered and destroyed. You can command the desolation to lift away and destroy the gates of hell in that place.

There is a doorway into the heavens called the astral world. In the book of Amos 5:8, the Bible talks about the seven stars:

"Seek him that maketh the seven stars and Orion, and turneth the shadow of death into the morning, and maketh the day dark with night: that calleth for the waters of the sea, and poureth them out upon the face of the earth: The LORD is his name."

Within the seven starts, issues of grave importance to man's existence are decided. This is what astrologers use to conjure spirits. People who practice transcendental meditations use them to conjure powers.

If you are involved in those things, you need deliverance. The covenant needs to be broken. If you have used occult books and meditated on them so much that they have settled into your soul, you need to submit yourself to deliverance.

Likewise, in the book of Isaiah 45:2-3, we read about treasures of darkness in the secret places (heavenly) places:

"I will go before thee, and make the crooked places straight: I will break in pieces the gates of brass, and cut in sunder the bars of iron: And I will give thee the treasures of darkness, and hidden riches of secret places, that thou mayest know that I, the LORD, which call thee by thy name, am the God of Israel."

The winds have their gates. If you look at the scriptures as recorded in Revelation 7:1, you will realize that the four corners of the winds are manned by four angels from heaven, not demons. Therefore, you can turn the winds against the forces of darkness.

Some of us have not read our Bibles deep enough to contact the spirit of revelation that reveals the mind of God to us. Consequently, this leads to ignorance in deep things of the Spirit. And because of ignorance, we are destroyed, terrified and cowardly run away from demons. We should not run away. When you want to undo any work of wickedness, you must do it according to the leading of the Lord.

There are times the Spirit of the Lord just comes upon you. Then, even without fasting, you can descend upon the enemy and dismantle spiritual structures that have been considered insurmountable. However, there are other times when the Lord will lay it upon you to declare a fast,. Please do so. For through the fast, God looses or unties the works of wickedness, as the Bible says in the book of Isaiah 58:6-8:

"Is not this the fast that I have chosen? to loose the bands of wickedness, to undo the heavy burdens, and to let the oppressed go free, and that ye break every yoke? Is it not to deal thy bread to the hungry, and that thou bring the poor that are cast out to thy house? when thou seest the naked, that thou cover him; and that thou hide not thyself from thine own flesh? Then shall thy light break forth as the morning, and thine health shall spring forth speedily: and thy righteousness shall go before thee; the glory of the Lord shall be thy reward."

This is not teaching you mysticism or magic or from my own imagination. It is from years of Bible study and seeking God's face about the mysteries of the Kingdom. At a time in my life, I got tired of being ignorant of the Word. I got tired of being battered by the kingdom of darkness. I got tired of being battered by witches and all those 'knowledgeable' people from

Eckankar, Rosicrucian, etc. There was I a university graduate, having my intelligence played upon by all kinds of people from the metaphysical world coming to tell me mysteries about metaphysics, scientology, etc., till I said, "God, break this from my life."

At this point I got tired of being a slave both to sin and to sinners. My friend, before it is too late, take the sword of the Spirit and set yourself free today.

When I rose up from my youth and saw opposition and wickedness abounding all over the place, I said, "God, this shall not be my portion." I followed the Lord and begged Him to show me the secret. And the Lord showed me things that shocked me.

It is because the powers of darkness understand the functions and dynamics of creation and they use them to release all manner of wicked things against us. The make their sacrifices upon those creations saying, "Creation, instead of releasing a portion to this man, steal from him, swallow from him, eat up his life."

Then, pour sacrifices upon each of these places. You will agree with me here that everything that God created has a mouth.

Unfortunately, they do not know the thought of the Lord in Jeremiah 51:44a:

"And I will punish Bel in Babylon, and I will bring forth out of his mouth that which he hath swallowed up:"

We can see in Genesis 4 that if you pour blood on the ground, the ground will devour you. It will strangulate you. Do you now see the essence of human sacrifices? They use them to open the gate (mouth) of the ground so that it can swallow up its inhabitants and resources.

Witches and wizards use mad people as points of contact and as a symbol of authority and power to control. They are like the mantle over a city. Having too many mad people in a city indicates that there is a lot of idolatry in that city. The more mad people we have in any particular city, the more the demonic authority and wickedness are there.

They are used by satanists as gates, as stepping points to accomplish their diabolical plans. When you pray, you need to pray for the mad people on the street and begin to tell God to break every manipulation of the power of darkness using these mental victims.

The Bible says every temptation has a door through which it comes to you. Hence, in every temptation, God opens a door of escape (1 Corinthians 10:13). The Bible says *"They shall come against me through one door, but they shall run away through seven doors"* (paraphrasing mine). You must begin to get sensitive enough so that when you begin to pray, you can pray specific prayers to break specific yokes.

In Isaiah 6:3-4, all that the angel needed to say when he was proclaiming toward the earth was, *"Holy, holy, holy is the LORD of hosts, the whole earth is full of his glory,"* after which the posts of the earth moved at the voice of him that cried. And the house where Isaiah stood to receive the revelation was filled with smoke.

"Holy, holy, holy, is the Lord of hosts: the whole earth is full of his glory. And the posts of the door moved at the voice of him that cried, and the house was filled with smoke."

The Bible speaks about the keys of heaven and the keys of earth. Two of the keys of heaven that God uses to open the mystery of the earth are **called praise and worship. We must have plenty of praise.** When you worship, doors open. Worship has a way of opening the door of the earth in particular. It is the language the earth hears readily.

From Isaiah 6, we have learned two things:
a)   **The earth has a door.**
b)   **Worship of Him that is seated on the throne can open doors.**

I challenge you to take up the armor of the Lord and deal with demons that trouble your life, wherever they may be loccated - in the astral world, on land, or in the sea. Command their gates to open in the astral world amongst the seven stars which are their headquarters of operation.

Stars have ways of controlling man. That was why when Jesus was born, His star was the sign that led the wise men to His place of birth.

"Where is Ho who has been born King of the Jews? For we saw His star in the east, and have come to worship Him" (Mathew 2:2 NAS).

Stars have a link to the existence of man. This is why some people can tell you "Your star will soon shine." But this is an astral language, not a scriptural one.

The astral world draws power from the stars. It is another gate that needs to be destroyed. When you speak about your portion, you must close up those gates. You must command them not to swallow you up. Pull them down. That is why the Bible talks about casting down imaginations of darkness that are put in the heavenly places. Therefore, you must cast them down.

One of the commonest entry points into a man's life that has for too long been taken for granted is having any property of the kingdom of darkness around or within one's house. If you have an image in your house that looks like Satan, it is a gate. Go and observe closely your art objects. It is time to bring out of your house things that look demonic and burn them up. If you are an art collector, get the right ones. I like decorations, but they must not look satanic. They must not be symbols of Satan. They must not be a labyrinth.

If you go to some people's houses, you may find amongst their items of decoration a picture of a snake with seven heads. What is it meant for there? That picture is a gate. It is an attraction for demons.

Do you have books on Eckankar or the Rosicrucian people or scientology? They are gates. Their presence anywhere calls forth an altar. They establish a meeting point for demons that will lurk around your house, influence your children and undermine your labor. Their presence around your house could be responsible for the present leakage in your life. Please get them out of your possessions and burn them up.

The day Samuel began to call the people back, they brought all the idols they had in their houses for Samuel to burn up:

"And Samuel spake unto all the house of Israel, saying, If ye do return unto the Lord with all your hearts, then put away the strange gods and Ashtaroth from among you, and prepare your hearts unto the Lord, and serve him only: and he will deliver you out of the hand of the Philistines" (1 Samuel 7:3)

When Paul preached, people brought out their idols to be destroyed:"

"And many that believed came, and confessed, and shewed their deeds. Many of them also which used curious arts brought their books together, and burned them before all men: and they counted the price of them, and found it fifty thousand pieces of silver" (Acts 19:18-19)

Until they were burnt, the spirits residing in them are not released. The gates are not closed. Prayer and anointing are not enough to close the gates. You must also burn them. When you burn them, you close the gates and expel the spirits from the items and also from your house.

Anything dedicated to Satan and kept in your house can form a gate that will attract demons there. It becomes a link and an entry point for Satan into your house. It may be a ring, a scarf, an earring or a pair of shoes, etc. You must demolish those gates. You must command them to shut up.

There are gates of heaven and there are gates of hell. That is why we sing, **"The Church is marching on... the gates of hell shall not prevail."** A detailed mention of the gate of heaven can be read in the book of Revelations. It was the gate of heaven that opened for Stephen in Acts 7:55-56 when he saw Jesus standing up there.

Even among heavenly altars, there are God's own altars that release His grace into your life. They are not built with physical things. God's altars on earth is in your heart. When you invite Jesus into your heart, He builds a covenant with you. He builds an altar and sets up His throne inside of you.

Wherever you find a throne, there is a gate. That is why all chieftaincy and high titles constitute gates. However, they can be made to represent either the gates of hell or heaven.

David was a king whom the Lord made to carry out priestly functions, meaning that his throne was established from heaven. That was why it was supposed to be forever through our Lord Jesus Christ who Himself came from the root of Jesse:

"Thy throne, O God, is for ever and ever: the sceptre of thy kingdom is a right sceptre" (Psalm 45:6)

This means there is a spiritual anointing that goes along with thrones. It could be from either Satan or God. Therefore, all our local chiefs and traditional rulers are either linked to Satan or to God.

You can decide for yourself which one you get yoked to Whichever you choose determines how and what you speak.

Now, when you speak about the altars and gates in the village, address the gates in the chieftaincy house. If you do not add that, you have not completed the attack. And if you can step into the place and anoint it as a point of contact, it is even better.

To whosoever you yield, you are a servant. Don't yield to any gate. They do not have any right to enslave or destroy you. Therefore, smash and throw them away. Jesus was sent that your soul might be redeemed. Christ has redeemed us from the curse of the law, for it is written, *"Cursed is any one that is hanged on a tree."*

Jesus became a curse that we may receive life. Now, your whole life can be renewed. It can be changed. You can throw away the yoke of that infirmity. You can speak unto the door by which that infirmity came into your life. You need the door of escape! I received my oil of deliverance through my door of escape.

Always use 1 Corinthians 10:13 in prayer which says, *"With every temptation is a door of escape."* When you pray, ask God, "Where is the door of escape from this infirmity? I receive my deliverance through that door of escape" When you put it that way, the altar of God will channel your deliverance. There is an altar of God in heaven that sits over the life of every saint. Actually, it is the altar of God in heaven that controls the life of the saints. Who is the priest of that altar? Jesus Christ. The Bible says He is seated at God's right hand that His enemies might be made His footstool. So, He is always ministering on the altar.

A NEW DIMENSION
Sorry, I feel led at this point to break the rules of writing, even at the risk of repeating myself or offending some readers by bringing you a summary of the teaching I gave to the body of Christ at the Ahmadu Bello Stadium Gymnasium, Kaduna just before the mass prophetic walk and prayer on all the gates and entry points in Kaduna.

The teaching seemed to have brought out in more explicit terms how God will have us understand the spirit of the matter of gates and prophetic prayer. It speaks of the heart of revelation of the conquering Church through prophetic praying that God has given me. It clearly shows God's way out for a world that is fast losing control.

I have only removed obviously unnecessary repetitions and left those with new dimensions of revelation that God has given as it is a very important part of our existence. God is fulfilling and effectively manifesting His power through us and in us in our environment.

Each time there is a consecrated groaning in prayer with fasting over a matter, God answers. In most cases where the answer is not negative and it has not appeared, even at the appointed time, it imperatively requires a kind of Jericho prophetic march and cry to pull down the walls and cause the answers to manifest.

As you pray and sing praises to God, He stores in you the power and anointing that breaks yokes. He makes it build to the measure of the fervency of your prayer. For your prayer power to be released and take hold of the situation, you need to go to the base of the situation - its root or contact point - stand over it and prophesy the answer of the Lord to it.

It is then that the effectual power of the Holy Spirit gets released through you to neutralize the situation, smashing through the veil or the smokescreen to make the answer visible, or create it where it did not exist. Until you release that power stored in you as result of your travail with God in prophetic prayer, some desperate life-threatening situations may never break.

"For it is God which worketh in you both to will and to do of his good pleasure" (Philippians 2:13).

"Now unto him that is able to do exceeding abundantly above all that we ask or think, according to the power that worketh in us" (Ephesians 3:20).

Transmit that power through the Rhema word (Bible in your heart spoken through your mouth) and the situation will catch fire, and the veil that holds back the miracle will melt.

Here is the teaching in Kaduna in northern Nigeria before the march in the city. Apply it to your life and let the Lord put you on the road to total spiritual liberation.

There has to be an entry point for any sickness before it can come into your life. Likewise, there has to be an entry point for prosperity to come into your life. It does not just come by chance. Something serves as the reason for your receiving a blessing

That is why God asked Moses, "Moses, what is that in your hand?" And he said, "God, it is an ordinary stick, an ordinary mantle." God told him to drop the rod on the ground and see what it would become. The rod turned out to be the miracle - the doorway.

The rod didn't look like anything capable of doing something extraordinary. Yet when Moses dropped it, it became a snake. He did not know a snake was in his hand. My friend, you don't know the miracle that is in your hand. You don't know the miracle that is in the environment. You may not know the mystery surrounding the environment until you have an encounter with God.

However, before addressing the gates outside, address the gates inside first so that you can approach the throne of grace with boldness. Jesus had to come down by himself because He is the key of life. The key of hell and Hades are all in His hands. He told Peter "Behold, I give you the keys of the Kingdon." These keys open all gates.

"And I will give unto thee the keys of the kingdom of heaven: and whatsoever thou shalt bind on earth shall be bound in heaven: and whatsoever thou shalt loose on earth shall be loosed in heaven" (Matthew 16:19)

What are keys used for? They are to open locked doors. There is no door the keys of the Kingdom cannot open. Where then, are the doors you should be opening? You know the doors that have been under lock and key against you. Therefore, start opening them now so that you can banish fear from you mind, and bodily fight the good fight of faith. After you've done this, you will live your life without any interruption from the powers of darkness.

Why do we go to the gates? Because gates are entry points from where cities, towns or villages are controlled. Secondly, it is at the entry point of every city that the covenant of that city is kept. Therefore, if you want to control the life of a city, one of the strategic places from where you can control it is the gate of the city.

The same pattern is also applicable to homes. If you are one of the privileged few who have a fenced house, the gate into that house, no matter where it is located, is the entry point into your home. Anyone who understands the spiritual dynamics and implications of gates may just come and say, "I shut up the gates of this house, and by this, I shut up the gates of the lives of those who dwell inside."

By this, he is using the gate of your house as a point of contact to the doorways into your life. It means any good thing you pursue in life will eventually elude you. That is why people sometimes wake up to find charms or concoctions at their gates. An enemy has done that.

Sometimes they cut the neck of a bird or any other animal and spill its blood at a person's gate. Or it may even be a charm that they would hang there.

I like what a former military administrator of Imo State did. While he was still new in the government house, he discovered that every morning, his family woke up to find amulets across the walls and at the gates, placed there during the night.

Cleaners would gather the charms and bring them to report what they had found that morning. Since they had swept and cleaned the surroundings the previous morning, they were puzzled why they should appear the next day.

Somebody was trying to lock up the occupants and control their lives from outside. The administrator was not accustomed to this kind of witchcraft and wondered where they had come from.

Being a child of God, however, he had to cleanse the whole government house by praying and anointing every part of it. He dedicated the house to the Almighty God. This stopped the operations of the kingdom of darkness against the occupants. Some other people have had to wake up to see strangers trying to take over their gates.

The whole of creation is shrouded in mystery. But thank God for Jesus! The Bible has helped us not only to be liberated but also to be able to settle down in life. Otherwise, some of these things will give us sleepless nights. This is why a lot of people, unable to unravel these mysteries, run from one sorcerer to another in the desperate desire to secure their lives.

I am taking pains to teach you this mystery so that you can confront life and death situations with revelation and boldness. We have not been given the spirit of fear but of power, love and a sound mind.

Now, let me show you two biblical examples. To have balanced teaching, I am going to give examples from both the Old and New Testaments.

"And he brake down the houses of the sodomites, that were by the house of the LORD, where the women wove hangings for the grove. And he brought all the priests out of the cities of Judah, and defiled the high places where the priests had burned incense, from Geba to Beersheba, and brake down the high places of the gates that were in the entering in of the gate of Joshua the governor of the city, which were on a man's left hand at the gate of the city" (2 Kings 23:7-8).

Why did the Sodomites choose to place the house of Satan by the house of the Lord? It was to counteract the altar of God. It was to oppress the altar of God so that they could slow down the work of the Lord. And, alas, the Church did not know what to do about it.

A grove is where satanic sacrifices, rituals and worships take place. Normally, it is always very close to where you have several trees, either in the wilderness or by the seaside. It is a meeting point for both demons and their human agents.

It can be worrisome to have somebody threatening to kill you for no visible reason - and not knowing what to do about it. It is not enough to console yourself with the fact that you've neither sinned nor stolen anything from anyone to warrant such a threat. It is a revelation of Jesus that will save you, not those consoling words.

Let us take another look at verse eight of 2 Kings 23 where Josiah was trying to carry out reforms:

"and brake down the high places of the gates that were in the entering in of the gate of Joshua the governor of the city, which were on a man's left hand at the gate of the city" (2 Kings 23:8).

This was the gate that led to the seat of Joshua, the governor of the city. Josiah had to break the shrines that were placed there in order to control him while in office.

Every ancient city has gates where sacrifices are made to control it. Ancient cities like Kano, Zaria and Benin in Nigeria have ancient gates through which their affairs are manipulated. At some of these gates, human beings are sacrificed as a covenant to sustain their satanic control over the city and afflict its inhabitants.

You will recall that there was one Gideon, an Igbo man who was killed in Kano for desecrating the Quran. They cut off his head and dripped his blood all over the city. It was a human-sacrifice deliberately made by the Muslims to secure the city and protect their religion, although many people thought it was mere vengeance.

Those who understand spiritual things and mysticism know that it was not mere vengeance. Otherwise, they would have simply hanged him and allowed his blood to spill on a spot. But to carry the head about with blood dripping from it was nothing short of a sacrifice to defend their religion and secure the land. Sacrifices of this nature are not peculiar to ancient cities across Nigeria and the rest of the world.

Past and present rulers of Nigeria, military or civilian, have made sacrifices to control the gates of Abuja. Their evidences are seen everywhere. While you are trying to behave like a nice gentleman, someone else has wrapped up your life and made you perpetually one step lower than him in the city.

He has locked up your portion and decreed that your portion must not compete with his. Therefore, when you should be the one spiritually dictating how the town should function, somebody degrades you and takes over from you. By this, they control the economy of the city.

In the Old Testament, when Joshua destroyed and conquered Jericho, he prophesied over the gate of the city:

"And Joshua adjured them at that time, saying, Cursed be the man before the Lord, that riseth up and buildeth this city Jericho: he shall lay the foundation thereof in his firstborn, and in his youngest son shall he set up the gates of it" (Joshua 6:26).

Many cities in Nigeria carry curses without knowing it. Kaduna in northern Nigeria is an ancient city. From the days of Lord Lugard, it has been a place of power. What happens in the physical tells you what has already transpired in the spiritual. For Kaduna to develop a "mafia" is an indication that there has been some level of control in the spiritual.

There have been strong covenants in the town, I believe that, to a large extent, these covenants regulate the affairs in the city. You will notice that only the "mafia" prospers in Kaduna. It is like they are sapping and drawing the energy and blood of every other resident to themselves.

Everybody else is working for them. They don't seem to be doing any real work. Yet they are unimaginably prosperous. Everyone labors for them: senior civil servants, big time businessmen, market women, artisans, etc. If you want any position, you have to lobby through this so-called "mafia." They have sapped the life of the whole city unto themselves. When you get to their gates, destroy their grip. We need to break their spell over the whole city.

As rulers make sacrifices at the gates of the city, they gather the life of that city - its wealth and everything - into their pots.

Chapter Three   47

It means that from then on, the wealth of that city must advance the work of Satan, obey his government and do his bidding.

That is why the righteous have to struggle so much before there is any breakthrough. But when the righteous begin to go to the gates to pray, the situation will change for the better, in Jesus' name.

Why was Lot not consumed in Sodom and Gomorrah - cities filled with adultery and all kinds of evil? The Bible says he always went to the gates to pray and travail. By so doing, he was uprooting the foundation of the people's grip over the land.

Those of us who have cars should create time out of our busy schedules as a matter of urgency, and take a ride outside the city to pray concerning our own matter and the city where we live, saying "God, each time I stay in this city, it is like something is trying to kill me. I feel like running crazy inside this city. Please release my portion there."

Then turn back, look into the city and command it thus, "O city, from your vantage position inside, live up your head in the name of Jesus that the King of Glory might come in."

In Acts 14:8-13, the Bible gives us a vivid illustration of how cities are controlled"

"And there sat a certain man at Lystra, impotent in his feet, being a cripple from his mother's womb, who never had walked: The same heard Paul speak: who stedfastly beholding him, and perceiving that he had faith to be healed, Said with a loud voice, Stand upright on thy feet. And he leaped and walked. And when the people saw what Paul had done, they lifted up their voices, saying in the speech of Lycaonia, The gods are

come down to us in the likeness of men. And they called Barn-abas, Jupiter; and Paul, Mercurius, because he was the chief speaker. Then the priest of Jupiter, which was before their city, brought oxen and garlands unto the gates, and would have done sacrifice with the people" (Acts 14:8-13).

What the priest of Jupiter was trying to do by offering sacrifices at the gate of that city was to establish the authority of Paul and Barnabas over the city. Evidently, authority is established over cities from the gate. Those people knew what they were doing. They were satanists who knew how the mysteries of these things operate.

You will notice that the priest of Jupiter came from outside to make sacrifices at the gates in order to exercise that control (though Paul had already been taken inside). If allowed to continue, this priest would have made Christians strangers, and they would have remained aliens to the city's power base.

Of course, depending on who is making the sacrifice, you can either be alienated or be brought into the caucus of the city-controllers.

What did God do to the Garden of Eden after He had driven out Adam and Eve? He set a sword of fire at the gate to prevent them from coming back and eating the tree of life. The gate established the authority of the city spiritually. This truth is consistent throughout Scripture, from Genesis to Revelation.

When you secure gates, you make every person outside your covenant an alien even while that person dwells inside. Because satanists have used their enchantments to secure city gates, they have made others outsiders, even though they are living inside the city.

This is what makes most city dwellers toil without any recognition from those in authority in the city. In the realm of the spirit, they are considered as outcasts. What a misery!

"Blessed are they that do his commandments, that they may have right to the tree of life, and may enter in through the gates into the city. For without are dogs, and sorcerers, and whoremongers, and murderers, and idolaters, and whosoever loveth and maketh a lie" (Revelation 22:14-15).

The above passage tells us that we don't go to heaven through the windows, but through the gates. Outside the gates are sorcerers and whoremongers.

That is why the Bible says in Psalms 24:6-8, *"Lift up your heads, O ancient doors."* Our generation is one that needs God. Our generation should have the gates to lift up their heads. The oppressor must not remain in our lives any longer. It is when you command the gates to lift up their heads that the King of Glory can step in.

When you release the word of God into it, the ground will open up. When you break their spell, there will be liberty in the land.

However, if the generation that needs God does not do this, it will remain in perpetual slavery and deprivation even in the midst of plenty. They will play second fiddle instead of being heads. Even when they come to the level of being heads, compared to other heads, they will still be slaves. *"If the son shall make you free, you shall be free indeed!."*

Each time the Old Testament saints entered a city, they built an altar. That altar was to open a gate, a doorway into that city to control the other gates that operated there.

It was to establish a covenant. Covenants establish altars for us. In the New Testament, whenever people made a covenant with the Lord, they were building an altar for themselves.

Until you begin to learn how to open your mouth and release the word of God from the inspiration and revelation you get from Him or from reading His Word against your situation, the gate controlling that situation cannot open.

When you open your mouth to speak, you are establishing the covenant of the Lord. In other words, you are establishing the altar of God in your life.

In Isaiah 38, when God pronounced a death sentence on Hezekiah, the king went back and declared a fast and began to beg the Lord to show mercy. The Lord had mercy and gave him back his life and even added fifteen more years to him.

Whereupon, he said the gate of hell had opened her mouth to swallow him. But God had shut up that gate. God can shut the gate of death against your soul so that it does not swallow up your soul prematurely. When you make covenants and pray to God, you can also ask God directly, "God, for these many reasons, I ask that you hold back the gates of death that they should not take my life."

No matter who may be manipulating a death sentence against you, it won't come to you because you have a covenant of life. When you are making a covenant of life with God, He will shut up the gates of death.

Death and the grave are two different things. Something abnormal is happening when you find yourself constantly involved in near-fatal accidents. It is a sure sign that grave is being used to draw your soul. It possibly means somebody has made a covenant with grave.

It is an intimidation from hell to subject you to perpetual fear. What you need to do is shut up the mouth of grave and command the doors to it be shut up. These are practical things that bring fear into people's lives.

There is also what we call the gates of hell. In Mathew 16:18, the Scriptures says that "...*upon this rock will I build my Church and the gates of hell shall not prevail against it.*" When every spirit you can think of seems to be pursuing you everywhere, when your business seems to be crumbling and your children are always falling sick, when hell seems to have been let loose against your life alone, it is the gates of hell trying to prevail to wrap up your life - to write off and cancel your ordinances on earth.

It means a conglomeration of the powers of darkness has been set loose against you through witchcraft. It is time to attack the gates of hell and tell Satan that, "It is written: the gates of hell - every head of darkness - shall not prevail over me. Therefore, I command that you let go of my situation."

But I must remind you that it is not every attack that you experience comes as a result of witchcraft. It may be just be an ordinary battle of life which Satan simply wants to use to test your faith without anyone instigating him. Of course, Satan often fights on his own without anyone asking him to fight you.

So please, you need not keep on suspecting your fellow human beings or being superstitious over everything that happens to you when you should be confronting your real enemy - the devil:
"*Be of sober spirit, be on the alert. Your adversary, the devil,*

prowls about like a roaring lion, seeking someone to devour. But resist him, firm in your faith, knowing that the same experiences of suffering are being accomplished by your brethren who are in the world" (1 Peter 5:8 NAS).

Even when the enemies come against you in their multitude, they shall scatter in seven ways. You will only look and behold their reward (Psalm 91:7-8).

Let me now move to the most beautiful one that has to do with our covenant.

OPEN THE GATE OF HEAVEN
Each time the patriarchs entered a city, they built an altar unto the Lord in order to make contact with the throne of God in heaven. This opened up the gate of heaven through which God lifted up His countenance on them. You remember the story of Jacob in Genesis 28, when he laid down in a certain place until he saw a vision. He didn't know that the place was the gate of heaven. When he finally came to full realization, he said, "Of a truth, this is the gate of heaven," and went ahead to anoint the place.

"Then Jacob awoke from his sleep and said, 'Surely the LORD is in this place, and I did not know it.' And he was afraid and said, 'How awesome is this place!' This is none other than the house of God, and this is the gate of heaven'" Genesis 28:15-17 NAS).

THE GATE OF RIGHTEOUSNESS
Both the gate of righteousness and the gate of heaven are the ones that give a person long life. *"With long life will I satisfy you and show you my salvation."*

"Open to me the gates of righteousness: I will go into them,

and I will praise the Lord: This gate of the Lord, into which the righteous shall enter" (Psalm 118:19-20).

That was the cry of the psalmist. It means that for the Lord to satisfy you with long life, the gate of righteousness must have sealed you up. Therefore, the gate of heaven and the gate of righteousness ensure that our covenant is kept alive.

THREE DOORWAYS
INTO THE PHYSICAL BODY

1. **The head**: Your head is a doorway into your body;

2. **The Eye**: Your eye is a doorway that helps your body to see outside and also facilitates entry from the outer world.

3. **The Breath**: Your breath is a doorway into your body. If people want to charm you, they can send their mystery through your breath. That is why in Job 27:3, the Bible says, *"The Spirit of the Lord is in my nostrils."*

These are doorways into the body.

There are some other doorways that are only outlets from the body. They don't take anything into the body, only send things out. Some of these are your hands and your legs. They are spiritual outlets that do not receive, but send out.

That is why the Bible says we should not lay hands on anyone suddenly. Likewise, you should not allow anybody to lay hands on your head because hands are outlets from the body and the head is an entry into the body.

If a man with a lying spirit lays hands on you, he will transfer legions of demons into the crown of your head, a vital center of your destiny because whoever takes control of the head has taken control of the whole body. The head is the control tower. Even when a person touches your head causally, you must protest if you are not sure of his spiritual standing.

This is a common practice during festive seasons in the village when, in the course of dancing and praying, people take advantage of the festive mood to touch others on the head. It is a means of imparting spirits. If this eventually happens to you, immediately plead the blood of Jesus to cleanse your head.

If you are an elder in the church, say of 50 years old and above, don't allow anybody to touch your head carelessly. The Bible says you are a Levite - you carry Levitical oil. The only person who can touch your head is a priest whom you are sure is spiritually sound and higher than you - not just any elder. You only subject yourself to a higher power. Even then, if you are sure that the priest is unclean, no matter how highly placed he may be, don't allow him to touch your head.

But if you know him as a servant of God through whom a lot of people have been blessed, let him pray for you. However, let him not touch your head because when he touches your head, both the clean and the unclean from him will enter your life.

When he only prays, because God has blessed him, it might favor you still. But when he touches your head, the things that constitute his personal life will mix with your oil. It is a spiritual thing. Don't take it for granted.

THE EARTH HAS A GATE (MOUTH)
The earth has a mouth (gate) through which it can swallow vomit and speak. In the old Testament scriptures, as recorded in Numbers 16, we read that the earth opened its mouth and swallowed the rebellious company that opposed the author-

ity of Moses the servant of God. The scripture below is clear evidence that we can command the earth to work in our favor and judge the powers of darkness.

Like in the Old Testament scriptures, stones came down to kill the enemies of Israel. These last days, stones will still come down to kill your enemies.

"And the serpent cast out of his mouth water as a flood after the woman, that he might cause her to be carried away of the flood. And the earth helped the woman, and the earth opened her mouth, and swallowed up the flood which the dragon cast out of his mouth" (Revelations 12:15-16).

DISSOLVE THE PALACES IN THE RIVER

Rivers have their own gates too. However, it is not only evil that comes from these gates. Neither am I glorifying Satan in this matter. You can take good advantage of them. Some gates can bless you. in fact, they are meant to be a blessing to you - only that satanists manipulate them against your life. When you use them for your own good, they're only serving their natural purposes. It is a natural creation meant to be used for different purposes.

We have spoken about the dragon in the previous chapter. Those who have dealt with sea demons often mention the queen of the sea and the queen of the coast. These demons are said to have palaces in the sea. If you want to capture a palace in the sea, command the gate of that river to open and the place will dissolve.

That is the law of the Scripture. Nahum 2:6 says: *"The gates of the rivers shall be opened, and the palace shall be dissolved."* After you have dissolved the palace in the sea, command the seven heads of Leviathan to be broken. Ask God in travailing prayer warfare to slay and break the head of Leviathan, that fleeing serpent.

"For God is my King of old, working salvation in the midst of the earth. Thou didst divide the sea by thy strength: thou brakest the heads of the dragons in the waters. Thou brakest the heads of leviathan in pieces, and gavest him to be meat to the people inhabiting the wilderness" (Psalm 74:12-14).

As many times as you do this you keep in check the workings of Satan in your life. Go a step further in your travailing prayer warfare and call for a hook in heaven to take the Leviathan (the dragon), bind and command the fishes of the sea to stick to his scales - demobilize him with that and ask the Holy Spirit to drag him out of the sea into the wilderness for the birds of the air to feast on him.

Finally, call fire from heaven to burn him. If you allow the Holy Spirit to fill you and stretch His hand against Leviathan (since you cannot), you will score a major victory in life's battle, and your life will find some ease. It is the Lord's battle.

"Speak, and say, Thus saith the Lord God; Behold, I am against thee, Pharaoh king of Egypt, the great dragon that lieth in the midst of his rivers, which hath said, My river is mine own, and I have made it for myself. But I will put hooks in thy jaws, and I will cause the fish of thy rivers to stick unto thy scales, and I will bring thee up out of the midst of thy rivers, and all the fish of thy rivers shall stick unto thy scales" (Ezekiel 29:3-5).

"In that day the Lord with his sore and great and strong sword shall punish leviathan the piercing serpent, even leviathan that crooked serpent; and he shall slay the dragon that is in the sea. In that day sing ye unto her, A vineyard of red wine. I the Lord do keep it; I will water it every moment: lest any

hurt it, I will keep it night and day. Fury is not in me: who would set the briers and thorns against me in battle? I would go through them, I would burn them together" (Isaiah 27:1-4).

This same method can be used to destroy the Leviathan's hold over nations, cities and governments, as he is the one that controls nations and directs governments through the waves of the air. He can stir up restlessness in nations by causing tumultuous spiritual waves to rise in the seas. The Church needs to seek the dwellings of God in order to keep Leviathan permanently bound.

If, peradventure, you one day find yourself in the midst of marine spirits - queens of the coast - where they try to manipulate you through witchcraft - close the gates of their rivers, discomfiture them and destroy their powers that the gates are bringing out. Then begin to command them to lift their operation away from your life. As you do this, their palaces, pots and powers in the rivers should begin to dissolve. This is the scriptural way of handling them.

You might occasionally find yourself in a dream surrounded by all kinds of witchcraft and marine spirits trying to lock you up. Command their gates in the rivers to lift up their heads because their powers are in the rivers. It is from there they draw their strength. Hence they are called queen of the coast.

If you are taking anyone through deliverance, use this method. Command the gates of the river where that demon came from to lift up their heads. You thus cut off the connection between the demon and her powers. Thereafter, command the palaces that give them life to dissolve.

If that person is truly from the river, you will see an instant manifestation. Some of them claim to be from the river when they are not. They only want to bamboozle and frighten you.

Every city created by God has a princely angel watching over it. Likewise, in every city there is a prince, like the one over Persia in Daniel 10:31:

"But the prince of the kingdom of Persia withstood me one and twenty days: but, lo, Michael, one of the chief princes, came to help me; and I remained there with the kings of Persia."

They watch over cities from the city gates which constitute a throne or a seat of power that rules that city. These strategic places carry authority that controls the life of the whole city. The reason why occultists go to the gate to make their sacrifices is to dislodge the angel in charge of the gate. They do this to set up their own counter-altar through which they call Satan their higher principality to drive away the angel of God seated there.

This is where you come in. If you are actively watching over your city as a child of God, that angel will not be driven away. Therefore, you need to exercise your authority over your city as a king and a priest made by Jesus Christ. Rise up and say, "Satan, who has authorized you to take control of this place? It is my Father's land. Our Father has not sold out the land to you. He has not ceded this country to you. So it should not be sold out."

When you exercise your authority, it will be difficult for any stranger to throw you out of your inheritance or take you for granted. Even when you are sleeping in your father's house and a stranger comes in to order you out, such a stranger can only suffer disgrace.

The real authority, the mantle of rulership, is within your

grasp. Use it! Jesus Christ did not die to only make you a joint heir. The Bible says He made you a king! This gives you the authority and mandate to operate supernaturally. He also made you a priest which gives you the legal right to partake of His divine nature and to manifest the mysteries of the Kingdom. Of course, what is the work of a priest? To lead people into their inheritance; heal the sick, raise the dead as he preaches the gospel of Jesus Christ, and reconcile them to God.

As a king and a priest, whichever way Satan comes against you, you can fight him back. If he comes by human authority, as a king, you have the legal right to stand and resist him.

If he comes with demonic authority, as a priest, you have the legal right to look at him and say, "I am the king and the priest here, get out! This is my kingdom. This earth belongs to me. It is written in the Bible that I am made to rule over everything that the hand of the Lord has created. Get out!"

The reality however, is that we often fail to exercise this authority. We live in fear as a result of ignorance of who we are in Christ Jesus. From today, don't be taken captive easily. What angels have been waiting for is to hear you call upon heaven to release them against those who want to rule the gates.

The people who invite Satan to take over those gates are human beings like you who were also given authority to live on earth like you. They have a right to the earth like you - only that they have chosen Satan as their own ruler. It is left for you to resist, and demand for God's rulership. And since the law that controls the earth is God's, He will take over from them. That is the advantage we have.

When Paul was arrested, he said while he was preaching in Jerusalem he was never arrested. But the day he came like a gentleman to pray and make offerings to cover them and the city of Jerusalem, they chose to arrest him.

YOUR DOORS SHALL REMAIN OPEN

Somebody once asked me if it is proper to relate with Muslims or to allow them to bless a believer with money or other material things. I answered the fellow in the affirmative. It is not only proper, it is very scriptural. You can accept things from unbelievers.

Only you must not steal like them. But when they bless you with material things and you doubt the source of the money, etc., pray over it. Except the Lord commands you not to accept it, you may receive it. If there is a snare attached to it to harm you, run for your life. God will command another well for you. Also, if it will defame the name of the Lord, don't take it. Outside that, please receive it, for "The sons of strangers shall build up thy walls."

"And the sons of strangers shall build up thy walls, and their kings shall minister unto thee: for in my wrath I smote thee, but in my favor have I had mercy on thee. Therefore thy gates shall be open continually; they shall not be shut day nor night; that men may bring unto thee the forces of the Gentiles, and that their kings may be brought" (Isaiah 60:10-11).

Dear reader, in verse 11 of the above scripture, note that the Bible uses the word gates. Just as there are many entry points into your body, there are also entry points into your house which shall be open continually so that people can daily transfer money, wealth and favor into your life.

Your own concern is to ensure that your gates remain open. When you pray, command your gates to open so that wealth may come in. Say, "Oh gates into my life, lift your heads into the heavens that the King of glory might bring me wealth."

Satanists can close your gates, but you can reopen them. The Scriptural command is, *"Therefore thy gate shall be open continually; they shall not be shut day or night.."* When your gates are shut against God, God cannot allow visitation to come upon you.

What are your gates open to? Your gates are not open directly to wealth. They are open directly to God who transfers the wealth. That way, He filters it. But you must keep it open continually for wealth to come in. You must keep open the altar of fellowship between you and God and always command your gates to remain open to blessings.

The above scripture says the gates shall not be shut day or night for men of every creed, nationality or color to bless you. It refers to men, not demons. *"... the forces of the Gentiles and their kings."* So when you pray, tell God to command men from the four corners of the globe to bring blessings to your house.

Angels are ever busy, day and night, transferring money from the central bank in heaven where the treasures do not dry up. God will command them to bring money, food, clothes and security, etc., to you.

"... That their kings may be brought" suggests that not only the men who will being blessings to you, but their kings also. My doors are open.

"Thus saith the Lord God, Behold, I will lift up mine hand to the Gentiles, and set up my standard to the people: and they shall bring thy sons in their arms, and thy daughters shall be carried upon their shoulders. And kings shall be thy nursing

fathers, and their queens thy nursing mothers: they shall bow down to thee with their face toward the earth, and lick up the dust of thy feet; and thou shalt know that I am the Lord: for they shall not be ashamed that wait for me" (Isaiah 49:22-23).

I look forward to the day when a prominent traditional ruler will visit my house with all the wealth of his domain. He does not need to be of the same faith with me. He does not need to serve the same God that I serve.

I have had a number of instances where a highly placed Muslim who would have fought me, helped me out of very tight situations. I was once reliably informed that one of the times when I was to be arrested in 1998, it was a very prominent Muslim in the State Security Service who stopped my arrest. The Lord will always come to protect me, cover me and defend me.

There are gates from your village that can pursue you to the city. If people invoke the soil of your village and curse you with it, they can use its gates to fight war against you in the city. That is why the Bible say, *"The gates of hell shall not prevail against us."* It is because hell can move from its foundation to wherever you are located and carry out its terrible intentions against you. Except you use the Word of God against it, it will prevail against you.

The entry point into the city - the border is where people are judged. Any day you are under pressure in the city, drive out in your car. When you drive outside the city, park your car in a corner and face the city and say "City, that which you are trying to steal from me, you will steal from me no more." You will thus break the yoke from outside the city.

When you feel you are being strangulated by the city, drive

out and say, "God, here am I. Let this strangulation go off my neck. Let the desolation go away."

In Ezekiel 11:11, the Bible gives us a timeless assurance:

"This city shall not be your caldron, neither shall ye be the flesh in the midst thereof; but I will judge you in the border of Israel."

The cauldron is where the flesh of the people in the city is cooked by satanists. They program you into all kinds of manipulations. They program your wealth and decide how much wealth should come to you. This is the work of the mafia. They constantly program the city.

As one set completes its diabolic assignment for the year, another set jostles to take over. In most cases, apart from programming one another, they program every other person to be a slave perpetually. They comprise the amazingly rich people in the city. The Bible says in Ezekiel 11:4, *"Therefore, prophesy against them ..."* That is the command of the Lord.

It takes watchmen to know these mysteries - people who desire to obey the Lord. I want to warn you that this may not be in line with the doctrine of your church.

But the truth remains that we are tired of being slaves in our environments. If the Son has set us free, we want to be free indeed. We don't decide to serve the Lord just because we like religion. If we had a choice, we would not go into religion, we shall serve Jesus.

Some people just want to be part of a church membership to fill a gap and follow a doctrine very strictly, then die and go to heaven. I would rather have the peace that Jesus said He had come to give us. If I could not find the peace, then I should not follow Him. I should look for it elsewhere. Thank God that the Bible is the Word of God that sets us free. Now that we have found the Word, we shall not be willingly ignorant. We would not choose to remain slaves.

"Surely I will no more give thy corn to be meat for thine enemies; ...Go through, go through the gates; prepare ye the way of the people; cast up, cast up the highway; gather out the stones" (Isiah 62:8, 10).

It is after you have done this that your labor for many years will yield dividends. I was preaching for about eleven years before our ministry started. We did not see the fruits gather the way they should. But as I began to carry this ministry in prophetic prayers, things started to take shape. Souls that got converted under our ministry began to stand the test of time. It was like the environment began to open up and gain people's attention.

When you go through the gates and establish this mystery upon the gates, you shall eat of what you have gathered in the city. When your children toil, they shall prosper also. Mystery will now open up and you will be blessed. Just be sure that you keep your own personal gates continually open for the Lord to let your blessings be to you.

Say, "Heavenly Father, I want to be translated from the ordinary to the supernatural, unto the dwelling of the Most High God. Every mystery of man that has entangled my life and tied me down as a slave because of the revelation of your Word, let it be broken now.

I call forth the Spirit of Life - the liberation that is in the Word of God - to break my yoke. For this reason was the Son of

God manifested that He might destroy the works of the dark kingdom."

The first thing you do after this is to ask God to reverse the curse by the blood. At the gate, you should confess the sin of the land and say, "God, we are sorry. There have been all kinds of incantations on this ground. There have been all kinds of sinful acts going on: fornication, adultery, murder, injustice, idolatry, etc.

Some of us were part of it. We are sorry, God now that our eyes are open. Restore our glory. Restore our liberty in the land, our authority and our inheritance, etc." Right there, cancel all other covenants that have been made with the pit of hell.

The second major thing you must do is destroy the cauldron at the gate and judge the town at the border. Destroy the cauldron, the works of every wicked man, including the princes of the land. These are the basic things we must do.

You may just gather the soil from the city gates. As you pray and prophesy over the soil in your hand, ask that those spiritual legislations on the land be reversed. When you finish, hold the soil towards the city, like Moses did against Egypt, and the soil became boils.

The third thing you are going to destroy is poverty. You are going to tell God that it shall no longer be spoken that somebody toiled and another person reaped. You will bring Isaiah 62 in fulfillment. It is the promise that goes with going through the gates.

The fourth thing you do is destroy all the blood covenants that Satan made over the land and which had subjected the land and its inhabitants to poverty and suffering.

The fifth thing you do is destroy the covenants of libations poured unto Satan and his demons such as wine libations, etc., which is the counterfeit of drink offerings that God commanded the children of Israel to bring before Him. However, in our dispensation of grace, Jesus Christ poured His blood as a drink offering to God which put to an end all forms of libations.

Lastly, destroy every form of idolatry in shrines. Every shrine is a gate. If, in your village, they still have the "Obi" that carries the family shrine, this is a gate to your village and a satanic doorway into your house. So, the day you go home, prophesy to it to spoil its power and legality over your family.

In Hosea 2:22, the Bible says, *"And the earth shall head the corn and the wine and the oil..."* One of the things that the earth hears and obeys is oil. When you go for evangelism, it is important that you carry anointing oil along to anoint and pray for the sick, and they shall be made whole. You would thus be fulfilling Mark 6:12-13:

"They went out and preached that men should repent. And they were casting our many demons and were anointing with oil many sick people and healing them." (NASU).

Please, always use the oil according to the Scripture to seal up whatever you have done. The oil of ordination is a physical symbol of consecration to God.

Every crossroad (intersection) is a gate used by satanists for different kinds of sacrifice. It is where they call for life - the breath of the spiritual current of that city.

If you have occult or Scientology books in your house, they are gates. In the book of Acts 19, Paul had to order the people of Ephesus to being out their magical books to be burnt.

Therefore, if you are a former Rosicrucian member, or if you just developed interest in reading their books, bring them out for burning. They are gates.

Otherwise, you will discover that you are not in control of the spiritual atmosphere of your house due to the presence of these books. They have the ability to attract astral powers.

As long as those books are there, they will attract demons because they are doorways through which the enemy causes leakages in your life. The Bible gives enough knowledge on how to deal with demons.

Therefore, don't just throw away the books. Burn them. By burning those occult books, you put to flight the power in them through the smoke. It is a sign of breaking the covenant. If you throw them away, their powers will still be present because you have not broken the covenant completely. If you want to break the covenant over your home, pray over them and burn them completely.

When you get to some of those intersections in the course of your driving, prophetically drive around them for a while and continue your journey. As you drive on, when you get to a gate, stop and take up a song of praise. "I will enter His gates..." Ask the gates to open to you.

You may come down there and continue the chorus of praise. With this, the problems that have been strangulating you will begin to soften and let go as a result of your command to the gates.

This is scriptural. According to Isaiah 60:18, the gates of your house should be called "praise." That means you should build your security in God by praising Him at the gates of your house. When you do this, Proverbs 14:19 will be fulfilled in your house.

"The evil bow before the good; and the wicked at the gates of the righteous."

This is what happens when a house is filled with hearts over-flowing with praise and thanksgiving. With it, you can pass decrees and uproot every wicked man in the city. It was at the border that God told Ezekiel to go and prophesy (Ezekiel 11:13).

Pelatiah died while Ezekiel was prophesying, and Ezekiel began to cry and say, "God, I didn't mean to kill them." He didn't know that was going to be the effect of his prayers. On the other hand, when Jeremiah prayed, he knew his prayer was going to kill Coniah. One year later, Coniah died and all his children died with him.

You need to understand that the spiritual exercise you are in-volved in is very lethal - it can heal. *"He shall be strength unto them that turn the battle unto the gates"* (Isaiah 28:5-6).

You must pronounce judgments from the gates. Therefore, whenever you are in a state capital, command all the gates in the state to lift up their heads. From there you also command the neighboring towns and cities not to influence the capital city negatively.. Their operations must not extend there. From there you can challenge all other gates in the other surround-ing cities and command their oppression to be lifted.

You must speak to the government house from the gates too. Use Romans 13 to command blessings to be released to the city and to your family.

You must control the gates in your city, your house and your personal life so that you can ensure a continuous flow of blessings for your business, ministry job and family. You must shut the gates through which Satan operates to control human affairs. Jesus secured for us the key with which we can open and no one can shut. And we can shut and no one can open.

"To the angel of the church in Philadelphia write: 'These are the words of him who is holy and true, who holds the key of David. What he opens no one can shut, and what he shuts no one can open'" (Revelations 3:7 NIV)

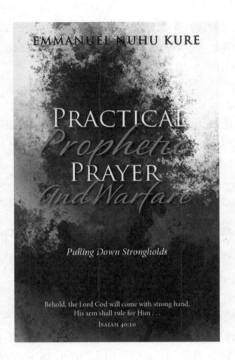

EMMANUEL NUHU KURE

PRACTICAL
Prophetic
PRAYER
and Warfare

Pulling Down Strongholds

Behold, the Lord God will come with strong hand,
His arm shall rule for Him . . .
ISAIAH 40:10

CHAPTER
4

CONSTELLATIONS

THE TIME FOR warfare has come! It is by spiritual warfare that Nigeria and the nations of the world are being daily divided and influenced. The war has gone beyond the spiritual realm. The Church must rise up to the standard of knowledge and revelation in order to be in control. If not, she will lose control. (No man who hardens his heart against God prospers, but worsens his suffering and oppression. Allow God to control your heart and you will prosper.)

Chapter Four

Even at the personal level, people are going supernatural to get things done. You had better rise up above the adversary or they will control you.

The Bible says that as a Christian, your place is not here on earth but in the heavenly places above principalities and powers. *"And hath raised us up together, and made us sit together in heavenly places in Christ Jesus"* (Ephesians 2:6).

It is from there that you are supposed to be ruling. If you see yourself down on earth, it means you have not made up your mind to go higher. Read your Bible and pray. Those who are ignorant of the efficacy of prayer must wake up from their slumber and learn to pray prophetic prayers.

Astral projection or exercise involves building a person's mind so that he can exercise inner power. In fact, in some parts of the U.S.A., early morning meditation is part of military training. Some military officers, serving and retired, are involved in astral travel. They hide under the guise of the New Age movement and even meditate in the White House to practice astral projection.

They understand spiritualism and astral operations. They control the elements in the air by telling the messengers in heaven to carry out assignments for them through astral projection. In the U.S.A, Japan and China, astral projection is used to enhance their citizens' productivity. Right now, Nigeria is going through an astral invasion of her life and systems using both traditional and modern methods.

By astral projections, I mean the mobilization of the inner powers (recesses) of the mind - transcendental meditation - to make contact with heavenly elements like she sun, moon and stars for selfish, manipulative reasons. It is then used to affect and manipulate the earth and its inhabitants.

The human mind is big and can imagine innumerable things. Most of our leaders are involved in mysticism and occultism. They find a common ground in this no matter their religious differences. It is through this avenue that they fight one another to govern the nations. Their minds and bodies are possessed. They enter into the occult to develop their minds and possess the gates and doors around them to advance these practices.

The world of sorcery which uses the air for war, operates in the astral world. The reason for the struggles and limitations in your life is that you are controlled by the astral world, both day and night.

Most religions of the world - Islam, Roman Catholicism, Buddhism, Hinduism and other Eastern religions are involved in astral manipulations through incantations, enchantments, repetitive prayers and songs. These religions possess and control the atmosphere by their repetitive enchantments and the burning of incense. Only prophetic pray encounters can destroy their spells. Any involvement in spiritualism is astral and is used to control lives.

Repetitive prayer, as against confessional prayer and tends more toward spiritualism and mysticism than true Christian worship. Anyone desiring to work and operate by the Spirit of God must understand this to be able to survive in this our generation. It is a worldwide threat. Take this warning from Paul to Timothy seriously:

"O Timothy, keep that which is committed to thy trust, avoiding profane and vain babblings, and oppositions of science falsely so called: Which some professing have erred concerning the faith" (1 Timothy 6:20-21a).

According to Ephesians 2:2, the devil is called the "prince of the air." Do you know that the air rules us today? He who rules the air controls the battles in military terms. The rulers of the Church's forces can be killed through air battles. Paul said we have been made to sit together with Christ in the heavenly places far above principalities and powers. We are above the astral world because He that sits above the astral world is God.

Whether you like it or not, as a Christian, you must live up to your calling or the situation will consume you. You must live a true Christian life. Satan is called "the prince of the power of the air" because when he controls the air, he rules humanity.

The air dictates the steps of the heathen. The wind that blows is not ordinary. Ezekiel was asked to call the four winds which are ruled by four angels. Right now, the four winds are being influenced against Nigeria. It is our business to stop this.

"Then said he unto me, Prophesy unto the wind, prophesy, son of man, and say to the wind, Thus saith the Lord God; Come from the four winds, O breath, and breathe upon these slain, that they may live" (Ezekiel 37:9).

The "prince of the air", the commander-in-chief of demonic forces, is the one by which the forces of the sun, the moon and the stars are mobilized to rule the earth against their original mandate. That is why Job 9:1-4 must be taken seriously:

"Then Job answered and said, I know it is so of a truth: but how should man be just with God? If he will contend with him, he cannot answer him one of a thousand. He is wise in heart, and mighty in strength: who hath hardened himself against him, and hath prospered?... Which maketh Arcturus, Orion, and Pleiades, and the chambers of the south" (Job 9:1-4, 9).

The above quotation is the summary of man's existence. Names like Arcturus, Orion, and Pleiades, and the chambers of the south are the ones controlling the stars. They are, in effect, the forces that control human existence. They can make life easy or terrible for you. Actually, the chambers of the south are the mysteries that unveil or carry the mysteries of the earth.

People involved in astral projections derive their power from there. When people go into yoga-type meditation which involves the folding of their arms, they go out of their spirits to call the elements from Arcturus, which are the harmonizing elements. Though they call its effect, "peace of mind," it is a kind of demonic possession from space.

Most of our older generations engage in this alien practice. When they start this meditation, they summon powers from the chambers of the south to harmonize their mind. What they do is conjure these elements into their soul to control them.

It is from there that they talk of projection. They either project themselves or project other things. They remotely control things in the seat of government and in other cities with the view to causing trouble and irritation among the citizens of the country, thus making them restless.

Occasionally, when you do something haphazardly and later wonder why you behaved abnormally, it possibly means somebody had been controlling you through an astral push. When you suddenly feel the urge to do anything, please check yourself or your liberties. You may be under their influence or manipulation. They can control things from anywhere because they are sorcerers, witches and wizards. They cause hatred, dissension and bitterness among people or between couples.

It is witches and wizards that help herbalists to succeed. Herbalists have to beg them to succeed. When herbalists make sacrifices, they hand them over to the devil. The prince of the air collects these things from them, programs the stars, and releases them to control their victims.

When the man you employed to take care of your business suddenly begins to misbehave, it is an indication that he is possibly under astral control. At this point, you need to be on your guard.

When you wake up in the morning or during the night and cannot read your Bible, it is possibly the influence from the Pleiades programmed to dampen your spirit. Every day, sacrifices are made to the Pleiades to influence people everywhere. Do you know that there are Muslims who read all the Quranic verses every day or repeat a particular verse throughout the day to establish a spiritual influence?

Similarly, by chanting for half a day, Hindus and followers of Guru Maharaji, send messengers to the Pleiades to oppress you. Don't lazily wake up to say, "I bind the devil." Rather than sit in your bedroom, learn to go to the place of battle and break their power over you.

The suffering of some Christians can be traced to the flimsy prayers they pray. The Bible says, *"Arise and shine, for your light is come and the glory of the Lord is risen upon you."* Rise up and shine because the day of your destiny has come. The sun shall neither smite you by day not the moon by night. You shall neither be afraid of the pestilence by day nor the terror that flies by night. Even though you walk through the valley of the shadow of death, you shall not be afraid of evil. For the Lord's rod and staff will comfort you. Amen.

The Spirit, the water and the blood are the three that can challenge the works of Satan on earth and in the air. Likewise, there are three that bear witness in heaven: the Father, the Word and the Spirit.

"For there are three that bear record in heaven, the Father, the Word, and the Holy Ghost: and these three are one. And there are three that bear witness in earth, the Spirit, and the water, and the blood: and these three agree in one" (1 John 5:7-8).

But our concern here are the three that bear witness on earth.

THE SPIRIT

The Spirit of life in Christ Jesus is one of the witnesses on earth against the astral world. Call forth the "Spirit of life in Christ Jesus" that sets you free from the law of sin and death to act against the chanting power. Romans 8:2 says, *"For the law of the Spirit of life in Christ Jesus hath made me free from the LAW (ordinances) of sin and death."*

Of course, the Bible says that the prince of the air perpetuates the law - the ordinance of sin and death. Note the word "air" is where the astral operates. It is a major arena of Satan because it controls the mind and every activity of man on earth.

It is in the air that Satan is worshipped. His subjects crowned him as the ruler of the earth, and they worship him as their god in the air. Hence, he is called the prince of the power of the air.

"Wherein in time past ye walked according to the course of this world, according to the prince of the power of the air, the spirit that now worketh in the children of disobedience" (Ephesians 2:2).

You must realize that the atmosphere around you always influences your feelings and emotions. That is what they work upon through astral projection. You need to invoke, invite or call the Spirit of life that is in Christ Jesus, which is the solution, to step into the atmosphere, clear them off and tear down the web.

This word "web" is important because they form a web in the atmosphere which makes your surroundings and feelings (emotions) uncomfortable. As a result, you find yourself iritable or losing your mind or doing stupid things and making mistakes. Jesus can clear them if you have Him in your heart and invite His Spirit to step into the atmosphere on your behalf.

THE WATER

The mystery of water baptism is that it is life. It speaks and bears witness for your soul in heaven. That which was earthly and had rights into your life has been washed through water baptism so the heavenly can rule. It is a declaration that the judgment of sin which was on you, even on earth, has been broken.

You can place a demand on heaven by declaring the baptism wherewith you were baptized into Christ must annul the sentence of hell on your head - and God will honor that demand.

Water baptism is a sign unto heaven and the earth of our redemption and Christ's ownership of our lives. The same Spirit that bore witness to men from heaven that Jesus is the Son of God, that men should hear Him (Matthew 3:17), still bears witness for all sons of God who have gone through or still go through water baptism by immersion.

The witness that spoke for Jesus will fight every witness from the constellations against us. It counteracts and cancels their ordinances that cry against us.

THE BLOOD

The blood of Jesus can scatter these powers in the air. The Bible says:

"And they overcame him by the blood of the Lamb, and by the word of their testimony; and they loved not their lives unto the death" (Revelation 12:11).

You must believe that the blood has legs - it is the life in Christ (Genesis 9:4). The blood of Jesus can walk into their realm and take captivity captive. The blood of Jesus is doing what Jesus did in the grave taking captivity captive.

One of the greatest weapons with which you can control the heavenly realms is the blood. Call unto the blood to step into the astral world in the atmosphere, into the Pleiades, and take their rulers, arrows and sediment captive, and clean up or blot out their ordinances, decrees and tie-ons against you.

Blood is not liquid when you call it. The day it dropped on the ground from the cross, it shook the earth and established authority on the ground. Thus, the ground has no right to disobey it.

By the virtue of the efficacy of the blood, the gates of hell had to open. Jesus broke through the gates of hell by the blood and destroyed all other contrary powers of death so that all that have lived under the shadow of death can be set free.

When you say, "the blood of Jesus," the Holy Spirit comes in between as a defense, a healer and a deliverer. The blood establishes redemption by picking you out of that situation because you were bought with a price, you were redeemed by that price. It is the Holy Spirit that carries out the functions of the blood.

SEEK HIM THAT MAKETH THE STARS

The Bible has commanded us in Amos 5:8 to:

Seek him that maketh the seven stars and Orion, and turneth the shadow of death into the morning, and maketh the day dark with night: that calleth for the waters of the sea, and poureth them out upon the face of the earth: The LORD is his name."

It is from the seven starts that the shadows of death, gloom, oppression, obsession, depression, poverty, suffering, etc., come. The Bible says, "He maketh the day dark with night; that calleth forth for the waters of the sea, and poureth out upon the face of the earth. The LORD is His name.

It is the Lord that you will seek to dislodge the elements. Your enemies are cooking and calling your name to affect your business, your mind and your sanity. If you experience instability in your mind, your business or intellect, tell the Lord to lift them. All these influences are from the Pleiades.

If you have their books - the 6th and 7th books of Moses, the 14th Chambers, the 38th Chamber, etc., bring them out to be burnt. If not, you are calling for the stars to disturb you and your business. Burning them is the surest way of dislodging the spirit fast. Or if you have their cassettes, don't keep them, do away with anything that belongs to them.

A song was recently released that echoes Allah, Allah and Allah for about a hundred times to cause people to sleep. Because the chants brought oppression, I began to pray against it. The chant symbolizes what happens in the air. Souls can be destroyed through chanting. We have to overcome by the blood the power in any sort of chanting.

Chanting generally has astral powers to project. It possesses the wind and releases the arrows of darkness to hold captive the environment. It fills the earth with satanic influences as part of astral projection. Chanting, enchantment, seances, palmistry, transcendental meditation, tarots, hypnosis and every other form of meditationistic activity and science of the mind are part of astral projection.

The blood of Jesus is one powerful witness that deals with them. Release the blood of Jesus to wipe them away. Invoke the water witness that separated you from the condemnation of the flesh and nature. The foremost of the witnesses is the Spirit of life in Christ Jesus.

Turn the three witnesses on earth against Satan in your environment, and the ground will break before you. You must learn to use the three witnesses in spiritual warfare. 1 John 5:8 says, *"And there are three that bear witness in earth, the Spirit, and the water, and the blood: and these three agree in one (God)."* Each bears witness for God on earth.

As a witness for God, water serves as the covenant for dew from heaven. It enables the labor of our lives to grow in spite of the hardness of the environment. This and the other revelations you read in this book are the means by which the Lord *"that strengtheneth the spoiled against the strong, so that the spoiled shall come against the fortress* (Amos5:9). May the Lord help us.

In Jeremiah 33:19-21, the Bible says God has with us a covenant that binds the day and the night:

"And the word of the LORD came unto Jeremiah, saying, Thus saith the LORD; If ye can break my covenant of the day, and my covenant of the night, and that there should not be day and night in their season; Then may also my covenant be broken with David my servant, that he should not have a son to reign upon his throne; and with the Levites the priests, my ministers."

Daily events and men's affairs are determined by what the seven stars release. The Bible says that the day the covenant of the day and night is broken, the covenant of our priesthood ceases to be.

It is time to take your place in God's divine presence through perpetual fellowship, prayer, waiting, free-flowing exercise, or release in the Word. It is time to take your place of authority on earth among the sons of God so that it can be spoken of you also that the Lord has sown you unto Himself on earth (Hosea 2:23).

Take note: a man's life span is the total sum of his days and nights on earth. The emotions he puts into those days and nights bring forth issues which are decided by the triangular power of the sun, moon and the stars which the Bible refers to as the powers of heaven.

In Genesis 1:16-18, the roles of the sun, the moon and the stars (the triangular force) are:
- First, they give light to the earth;
- Second, they rule over the day and night; and,
- Third, they divide light from darkness.

"And God made two great lights; the greater light to rule the day, and the lesser light to rule the night: he made the stars also. And God set them in the firmament of the heaven to give

light upon the earth, And to rule over the day and over the night, and to divide the light from the darkness: and God saw that it was good.."

In the whole of creation, the sun, the moon and the stars are the only ones given the mandate to decide what happens in the day or in the night. That is why the Bible says the sun shall not smite you by day or the moon by night.

They decide whether it is well with you or whether it shall be bad with you. They control the times, the seasons and the days. That means that they control the atmospheric conditions which, in turn, affect our lives. Those same conditions allow us either to live long or die young.

The triangular power of the sun, moon and the stars have creative powers in them to make things happen. They were meant for signs and wonders. *"And let them be for signs, and for seasons, and for days, and years"* (Genesis 1:14b). These decide man's destiny and how long he lives. They can call forth poverty, plagues, pestilence, pain, death, sorrow, joy, prosperity, peace, health, etc. Hence, the Bible refers to them as the powers of heaven, against which it assures us *"The sun shall not smite thee by day, nor the moon by night'* (Psalm 121:6).

It is from within these elements that the astral forces attempt to operate their powers. Both the learned and the illiterate refer to these powers as astral powers. But the Bible refers to them in covenant words as the powers of heaven.

Prophecy, generally and loosely used means time. Prophecy therefore, relies on these triangular forces as a vehicle to fulfillment. It controls the worth and quality of man and the whole of creation. This is why the Bible gloriously proclaims: *"... worship God: for the testimony of Jesus is the spirit of prophecy*" (Revelation 19:10b).

This means the testimony, the proclamation and the word of Jesus Christ is the only life (Spirit) that controls the powers of heaven. Jesus, therefore, is the ONLY KEY to unlocking the powers of heaven and their emotions. That is why the saints must arise and ensure that the powers of heaven speak to affect every imbalance in power and ensure prophetic exactitude at the coming of our Lord Jesus Christ.

"And there shall be signs in the sun, and in the moon, and in the stars; and upon the earth distress of nations, with perplexity; the sea and the waves roaring; Men's hearts failing them for fear, and for looking after those things which are coming on the earth: for the powers of heaven shall be shaken" (Luke 21:25-26).

With the release of this revelation to the Church, the day of God's glory through the Church is at hand. It is time to put on our priesthood, which is in Christ Jesus, and break the veil of life that has limited us.

The stars fight their courses according to their powers and strength. They array themselves in battle formation when the covenant of God is threatened, and there is a cry: *"They fought from heaven; the stars in their courses fought against Sisera"* (Judges 5:20).

Something must be missing in our daily spiritual warfare which prevents the heavens from fighting for us in their different glories.

"There is one glory of the sun, and another glory of the moon, and another glory of the stars: for one star differeth from another star in glory" (1 Corinthians 13:41).

In Revelation 1:16, Jesus had in His hands seven stars, not a sword - the instrument of His perfect control of the power of the heavens. Each star was an angel of the Church. It was His mouth at work, not His hands and the sword.

With the stars in His hands and the sword in His mouth, He fought and won His battles. Oh, that the scales would fall from our eyes so that we may behold the mysteries of heaven. May God translate you into the likeness of Christ.

If you must control your environment, the atmosphere and the things that happen to you, you must take charge of the realm of the stars by prayer, purging their influences from the lives of men. You must break the snares of satanists; the ordinations and the ordinances made against you and locked up in the stars.

For the enchantment of every herbalist, medium and satanist to work, they manipulate the senses and influence the Pleiades to carry and store up venom for their prey - whether that prey is an individual, nation or thing does not matter. However, as long as that sediment and altar in the stars are not built, they cannot afflict or affect their victims.

It is like the cauldron being built in the stars (Ezekiel 11:11). After consulting for their clients, they invite Satan and the powers of darkness in the night to institutionalize in the stars their evil so that it can rule men's lives. It is this evil that the Bible says must be broken in the stars. You must break it to render their incantations powerless.

"Though thou exalt thyself as the eagle, and though thou set thy nest among the stars, thence will I bring thee down, saith the Lord" Obadiah 4).

One discovery that continues to agitate any mind is the fact that some of the stars are actually God's angels in the form of stars. Can you imagine yourself looking up at the stars in the evening and imagining that some of them could be angels looking back at you? Great are the wonders of the most High God!

In Revelation 1, it is written that the stars in His hands were seven angels. In Judges 5, the stars fought in their courses. And in verse 23, an angel cursed Meroz for not coming to help Israel.

"Curse ye Meroz, said the angel of the LORD, curse ye bitterly the inhabitants thereof; because they came not to the help of the Lord, to the help of the LORD against the mighty."(Judges 5:23).

May they curse those things that do not help you in the day of your trouble. That angel must be one of the stars that fought in their courses. This means that angels sit directly over you, watching you sleep in your bed at night. This should make you sleep well, knowing that, like watch dogs, there are eyes watching and monitoring your environment even in your subconscious state of sleep - eyes to act if there is a breach of covenant from hell.

It means that when you walk around, angels keep track from behind the stars. Your part is to keep fellowship with the Father. Their part is to keep watch over your life for the Father.

Therefore, feel free to command them in the name of Jesus Christ to act for you in emergencies after letting the Father know. The seven stars in Amos 5:8, therefore, are seven angels who under the command of God, watch over the heavens and the constellations to clear it of death, oppression and evil against the Church.

They turn shadows of death into morning, releasing and maintaining the sweet influences of Pleiades and the powers of creation into our lives, our homes, our families and our jobs.

The beauty and the glory of this oversight are summarized in the symbolic woman in Revelation:

"And there appeared a great wonder in heaven; a woman clothed with the sun, and the moon under her feet, and upon her head a crown of twelve stars" (Revelation 12:1).

No wonder the earth came to her aid in Revelation 12:16 because the earth gets her signals from the heavens:

"And the earth helped the woman, and the earth opened her mouth, and swallowed up the flood which the dragon cast out of his mouth" (Revelation 12:16).

May the earth and the heavens catch your signals from the throne. May you rise up from the valley and take your proper place on earth and in the heavens. It should not be mentioned that you were rendered helpless because some enchantments, initiated from the pit of hell, directed the sun, the moon and the stars to prevent you from reaching your destiny.

The battle is the Lord's. All you need to do is apply the principles of warfare correctly and you will remain a victor all the days of your life.

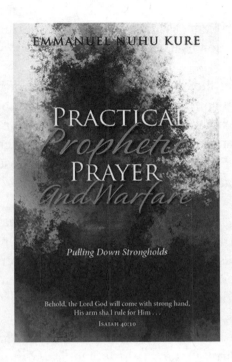

EMMANUEL NUHU KURE

PRACTICAL
Prophetic
PRAYER
and Warfare

Pulling Down Strongholds

Behold, the Lord God will come with strong hand,
His arm shall rule for Him . . .
ISAIAH 40:10

CHAPTER
5

THE SPIRIT OF ADOPTION

WHEN YOU ADMIT your infirmities, the Lord covers you. But when you do not accept them and think you are alpha and omega, you will remain vulnerable all your life. You will wake up one day and find yourself lonely without a church and without a friend.

Any man who is ready to admit his infirmity is ready to establish the Kingdom of God. There is no man without infirmity.

But it is the brokenness that goes with that infirmity that draws God to the person as a cover.

Have you ever thought that something good or bad might be following you spiritually even though you are born again? It might be an inherited thing. Timothy's grandmother was a woman of transparent faith, a powerful believer in the Lord Jesus Christ. So also was his mother, a grandiose woman, "A mother in Israel."

The fact that Timothy himself became a spiritual giant under Paul testified to the fact that he drank faithfulness from his mother's breast. No wonder, Paul made reference to Timothy's unwavering faith which he inherited from his mother Eunice and grandmother Lois.

"When I call to remembrance the unfeigned faith that is in thee, which dwelt first in thy grandmother Lois, and thy mother Eunice; and I am persuaded that in thee also. Wherefore I put thee in remembrance that thou stir up the gift of God, which is in thee by the putting on of my hands" (2 Timothy 1:5-6).

Have you ever thought that what you are today could possibly be as a result of what you drink from your mother's breast? Have you ever wondered why Paul, a great man of faith who opened up mission fields had to say, *"Oh wretched man that I am, who shall deliver me from this flesh of sin?"* May you today not pretend to be holier than you truly are so that the Lord, in your honesty, might set you free to function under the power of His holy oil (anointing).

In Zechariah, we read about the two witnesses. They were human beings whom the Bible calls two witnesses that stood before God as olive trees. Do you know that the day you become perfectly conformed to the image of Christ as He takes you from glory to glory, you become in heaven an olive tree that pours oil?

This means your life becoming oil, an instrument to lubricate the lives of men on earth. Do you know that in heaven, the woman is like oil? Do you also know that the woman is the wedding ring between God and man? Do you know that a woman can make or destroy a man?

The Bible says that the two witnesses, though human beings, were olive trees. When the devil and the entire realm of the spirit looked at them, they saw two olive trees. It simply meant they were the life of God on earth.

The olive tree is the life God released into man. We use olive oil because the tree in heaven is recognized to be an olive tree which supplies the olive oil. That is why we do not use ordinary "ororo" (vegetable oil). We can only use it as an alternative when olive oil is not available at that particular time. If olive oil is available, we do not use vegetable oil. It is not an alternative in heaven. Therefore, it can only be an alternative amongst men.

The Bible is very strict about the instruments of sacrifice. You do not use just any instrument for sacrifice. If you are using a lamb, it has to be a lamb without blemish, with no freckles. Though lambs may look alike, in the Scripture, perfection is in order. If it is an olive tree in heaven, it must be olive oil on earth.

We should beware of irrelevant doctrines. Even if you saw anything in a vision that is not scriptural, it is your vision and not the Scripture's. Anything that is not scriptural is not of God.

Our faith becomes perfected when we strictly follow scriptural principles. By this, we become invisible, untouchable and proof producers. It is the "extras" that we add that render us vulnerable. Do you want to know the secret of perfection? Stop adding extras to the Word. Stop allowing your pride to interfere with God's work. God has no pleasure in the proud.

In Genesis 48, when Jacob was very old and about to die, he went to see Joseph. There, he began to transfer a mantle anointing. Interestingly, the first two people Jacob transferred the anointing to were strange people (Ephraim and Manasseh).

"And Jacob said unto Joseph, God Almighty appeared unto me at Luz in the land of Canaan, and blessed me, And said unto me, Behold, I will make thee fruitful, and multiply thee, and I will make of thee a multitude of people; and will give this land to thy seed after thee for an everlasting possession. And now thy two sons, Ephraim and Manasseh, which were born unto thee in the land of Egypt before I came unto thee into Egypt, are mine; as Reuben and Simeon, they shall be mine. And thy issue, which thou begettest after them, shall be thine, and shall be called after the name of their brethren in their inheritance" (Genesis 48:3-6).

I want you to observe the contradiction in verse 5:

"And now thy two sons, Ephraim and Manasseh, which were born unto thee in the land of Egypt before I came unto thee into Egypt, are mine; as Reuben and Simeon, they shall be mine."

Have you seen the trouble there? Suppose you have children and I am your father. I pick two of them and say, "These are no longer your children. Today I adopt them as my own children." What would your children become to you? By the law of adoption, they would become your brothers, of course. Is that not an abomination in any culture? Little boys becoming equals with their grey-haired father!

This may be an abomination on earth, but it is the mystery of heaven. And that is why if I say you are older than Satan, you had better hold your head high.

That is the mystery of the spirit of adoption. When the devil attacks you, tell him that you are not in his age group. You are older than him and he should shut up. Tell him to stop disturbing your peace. Do you know that the spirit of adoption has made you a joint heir with the Lord Jesus Christ? Before Satan was, Jesus was - and will continue to be.

In Ephesians, the Bible says that before the foundation of the earth, the Lord had me in His "stomach."

"According as he hath chosen us in him before the foundation of the world, that we should be holy and without blame before him in love: Having predestinated us unto the adoption of children by Jesus Christ to himself, according to the good pleasure of his will" (Ephesians 1:4-5).

Therefore, when God was creating Lucifer, who later became Satan because of rebellion, He was doing so for me, so that Satan could eventually serve the two of us. If God already had your pregnancy while He was still creating somebody else, who then is older?

You, of course! You were already in Christ looking at Satan while he was being created. Similarly, Jeremiah 1:5 and Psalm 139:15 say that you had existed in the secret place before you were conceived in your mother's womb. That too is a mystery of God which I want you to catch very fast. It means, by the spirit of adoption, God has made you older than Satan.

Normally, in the order of age, you start by blessing the first son, but since Jacob started with Ephraim and Manasseh before coming to their father, he had exalted them above their father. This is a very serious matter in heaven and I want us to treat it with the same seriousness. Why did Jacob have to adopt Ephraim and Manasseh?

Since they were made equal to Reuben and Simeon, who were older than Joseph, it meant that from that day, the children were also older than Joseph - at least in manifestations of the oil in their lives. May you pass that blessing to your child in Jesus' name.

Where Israel said, Oh God of Abraham, Isaac and Jacob" a miracle happened up till now in accordance with their covenant with God which He cannot break. It is like praying in the name of Jesus. The names of these patriarchs have become covenant names in heaven which God cannot break.

That day, Jacob was transferring covenant blessings on Ephraim and Manasseh. He was not only making the children equal with and older than Joseph their father, he was making them equal with himself as well. It means the same oil that secured the names of Abraham, Isaac and Jacob also flowed upon their children.

The original oil that grafted me and made me a part of the multitude is the original oil that propelled these children. That is the spirit of the perfect. No wonder Ephraim had a watchman with God. Hosea would say, "And the watchman of Ephraim was with my God." The angel of Ephraim dined with God day and night as Ephraimites had easy access to the Most High.

Why did Jacob do what he did? There is an order in heaven that none of the covenants of the Lord Almighty must be broken by marrying a person outside the covenant. While in Egypt, Joseph married an Egyptian woman and violated the covenant of his God.

If Jacob had not done what he did, which spiritually changed their nationality, the children would have carried the blood of Egypt throughout their lifetime - thus carrying the Egyptian character which was an abomination unto the Lord. By birth, they had inherited from their mother the poison of Egypt and the evils of the gods of Egypt. This presupposes, apart from Joseph, that from their mother to all their children, all others were condemned to hell. By this, Joseph would have been leading a family of demons.

Jacob was determined to retain a remnant in the family of his son Joseph. Hence he stepped in. Zipporah too, in her own case, knew that the only way she could save Moses' life was to cut off the foreskin of their child and throw it away. Jacob knew in the spirit that the only way he could save that remnant for the house of Joseph was by directly translating a sample of Joseph's blood, adopting it into the main blood stream of the original covenant in heaven.

He was grafting them into the oil of Melchizedek - into the priesthood that never fails into which he had already been grafted. Abraham and Isaac had already been grafted into the same covenant. That is why there are three names. Whenever Israel prayed in these names, miracles happened.

These children of Joseph were the most fortunate on earth - grafted suddenly! It meant they could operate spiritual powers more than their fathers, and understand God more than Simeon an Rueben since they were now directly linked to the eternal order of the priestly oils of our Lord Jesus Christ above their father. It was like Paul who came late and got grafted in but carried the oil more than the disciples who sat and ate with Jesus.

Some blessing by which the Lord said you shall multiply and fill the earth were the same blessings he put upon them. What God told Abraham, Isaac and Jacob was what Jacob transferred to the children of Joseph - Ephraim and Manasseh. It is a mystery of God.

Maybe you do not understand what I am saying. It is possible to be born again yet still have the oil of Egypt speaking in your life. Until you appear before the Lord to cut off that oil, the oil shall control you. This is because that oil was naturally inherited from the womb of your mother and from the loins of your father.

When a child resembles neither the father nor the mother, there's bound to be some query for the mother who may be asked by the father to explain the source of the strange baby. Every child picks one trait or the other from both parents. A temperamental child or one who lies often, for instance, must have taken the trait from one of his parents.

In the Old Testament, God said He gave birth to children that did not look like Him. It is possible for you to be a child of God without looking like Him. God always gives His legal children His identity so that when the devil sees them, he will see in them the original oil of His perfection.

When one of my younger brothers was very small, he terrorized every other child in the neighborhood. My father tried all he could to tame him but to no avail. At the end, he had to send him to Kano to live with an uncle whom he was sure would effectively tame the boy. About seven years ago, I got really concerned and asked my father who, between him and our mother, was the terror. He said neither of them, but our grandfather was.

Our grandfather is said to have come from a clan of warriors that always succeeded in defeating the Hausa-Fulani invaders. He and other warriors always returned home from war with the heads of their enemies as a sign of victory. When I understood that mystery, I got the whole immediate family together (including our father who is born again) and grafted all of us out of the wild olive tree into the spirit of adoption into Christ Jesus.

The wild olive tree must die. You must be grafted today. There has to be a grafting before there is a dedication.

If nothing that you touch ever goes far, despite sustained prayer and fasting and deliverance sessions, the cause of your problem may not be demons. It mat be something you sucked from your mother which the devil may be using to manipulate your life. This could possibly be a genealogical transfer of wild olive oil of affliction rooted in your ancestry and which has become a characteristic in your life. Unless you address that situation, it may prevent you from breaking even or eventually kill you.

For some, it may be an inherited family curse. Some family quarrels may have been transferred to the children who have taken the fight to a diabolical level, cursing one another and the land. I have witnessed an instance where a family quarrel lasted through four generations. The curses invoked by one generation haunted coming generations.

If anointing oil is poured on you while your vessel remains

strange, the oil will kill you. The day unrighteousness carries the oil of God it dies, for God is too holy to behold by iniquity. You must have heard the story of the old wineskins which burst with the new wine.

May God destroy your old wineskin. This is what I am asking you to do today. I did it several years after I was already a popular minister. I was not ashamed of it. Pride remains the greatest undoing of most people. Ask God to first deliver you from the spirit of pride.

You must remember that in Numbers 21:9, even while the serpents were biting people, some of them preferred to die than look at the golden serpent. May you be delivered from this spirit.

Is there any trait in your life that is giving you an image that is detrimental to your faith or ministry? I want you to look deep into yourself before you pounce on all the demons of the earth. Did your father have that trait? If you find out that your father had it, destroy the wild oil from your father.

It is after this that you can stop outer demons. As long as you fail to do this, no matter how hard you fight the demons, they will keep coming back to you because you have provided them a legal ground to attack you. We need to understand the legality of the realms of the spirit.

A man who speaks irritatingly slow may have taken it from his father. If a man who stammers has no precedence within his family (paternal or maternal) up to the fourth generation, then there is a likelihood of demonic oppression. If he can cast it out, he will be delivered. However, if he finds one who is in his lineage, he should check the family bloodline - the wild olive oil could still be running through the family. Once he breaks it, he shall be delivered from his stammering. If you are one of those who carry a sickness that is common among their family members, today you can cut off that branch in Jesus' name.

My father worked with the Nigerian Ports Authority for many years. During that period, he remained in one position for more than eight years until my mother advised him to resign. Still, my father tarried on the job. However, the day he finally made up his mind to resign, he was promoted. From that time, his promotion became regular. But the fact remained that he had lost so many years during which many of his friends and colleagues had moved way ahead of him.

My father would obtain money to buy a car, come home to show us the money, and that night we would celebrate by eating the last chicken in advance of the car to be purchased. But just as we said our ten pm prayers and were about to retire to bed, someone - often a very close relative - would come knocking on our door.

The fellow might have arrived by train that night from Lagos. While we retired to bed after receiving him, he and our father would stay awake till the early hours of the next morning discussing. Early in the morning, the two of them would leave the house. Then, very late in the night, our father would return with his head bowed in shame for the sin he had committed.

He had given the money meant for the car to his guest who must have gone back to his base with the money meant for our car. Our hope of getting a family car had been burst again. As this happened quite often, we grew up loathing our father.

It was as if somebody told those unexpected visitors that our father had just collected money for a car. Then they would come to lift the money off him. This trend continued for a long time. Besides, crisis situations began to create themselves soon after his retirement. These saw him selling off all the houses and plots we had in Kaduna.

The first time he did that, I came home from the university and said, "Please, sir, don't sell the house again. If you keep selling them, where shall we stay when we come out of the university." He said, "My son, it was my sweat that built this house. When you come out of the university, your sweat will build your own house." Then I would return to campus feeling really sad and bitter. Then the one I called the rebel in the family a few years ago would rant on my father saying; "I hate you, you ruined our lives."

My father was far from being a poor man. He built houses. But all the houses were sold out after his retirement. I built the house he is living in now so that I could have a blessing for eternity. I did this to wipe away the curse of his wild olive oil. I wanted to make restitution for him.

But thank God about seven years ago, my father realized his error, and he apologized for all he had done. From then on, he lifted away that reproach from our lives. "My children," he said, "my mistakes shall not be your mistakes. My pit shall not be your pit. This day, I lift away that curse in the family. I lift away that wild oil." He made restitution that day and prayed for all of us.

Is that not the pattern that is taking place in your family? Is that not the pattern your life is gradually following? What is your own family olive oil? If it is a wild olive oil, it has to be broken now! Stop grumbling and complaining about your husband or wife. Attack the root - the wild olive oil. You know your weakness. Don't allow other men to drive a sword through your heart. Attack it by yourselves.

When you judge yourself, no man shall judge you again. The Kingdom of God suffers violence. Therefore, arise and take your destiny by violence. If you dare touch the soul of your Father in heaven concerning a matter today, your destiny will be established.

"For if thou wert cut out of the olive tree which is wild by nature, and wert grafted contrary to nature into a good olive tree: how much more shall these, which be the natural branches, be grafted into their own olive tree?" (Romans 11:24)

Your father is a tree and you are his branch. Note the word is present tense - factual - which means the wildness of your father continues forever until you are cut off from it. Because it is a trait in the family, it will continue to follow your own children until you cut it off from them.

Each time I look at my own children, I say, "You will not be as foolish as the oils in your father's family, nor will you inherit the traits of your grandfathers." From today, like Jacob said, "That which God blesses me with, the covenant, I transfer unto you."

Every year I renew the covenant of my children. On the birthday of anyone of them, I call the celebrant to kneel down. Then I call their mother and other members of the family present to stand around in agreement. Together, we pray for the celebrant by cutting off the wild olive tree and every evil trait. Then we bless the child and release him / her into prosperity.

Thank God, my children are not taking my traits. They are peculiar children in the sense that those things I could not do at their age they can do. I could not correct myself. But they correct themselves. I had to learn it with oil. But they do it so easily as if they were born with it. It means that, right now, they are growing under a new law and a new principle.

What we are saying here is that you must be grafted contrary to that olive oil in your father's family. When Jesus adopted you by the spirit of adoption, He did it so that you might go contrary to nature. Incantations and ordinances are part of your natural environment. But you were born again to walk against them to live your life contrary to incantations. When you do, incantations can never take you captive.

Some people are slaves to the wild olive oils in your families. They lack their own identity that could position them out of the family. Perhaps, your mother did not have a husband. Up till now, you do not know who your father is. It is part of your secret. It is part of the secret of your family. Because you came out from a background with no identity, your life will continue to float in the air. You become like a fugitive whom everyone can exploit and plunder at will. You must break the wild olive oil.

A beautiful, highly sophisticated sister met me in a Full Gospel Businessmen's Fellowship International (FGNFI) gathering a few years ago. She was the type one could refer to as self-made. As a major sponsor of her own chapter of the Full Gospel Businessmen's Fellowship International, she had a fleet of cars.

But amidst tears this sister told me her problem - she could not get married. I was shocked. Thank God, she met me in a hotel room together with the president of the chapter who was equally worried. He told me that all the top deliverance ministers invited to the meeting had taken the sister through deliverances without any positive result.

When I heard the names, my heart sank. I said, "God, can this one ever be saved? She must be a demon incarnate. If all these men of God have prayed over her to no avail, something must be wrong." Meanwhile, she continued weeping.

Not knowing what to pray again, I got confused. I did not want to join the list of ministers who had prayed and failed. I said, "God, where is the answer?" The Spirit of God came upon me and said, "My son, don't despair." As I inquired further, I learned she got born again some years ago and was an 'angelic' sister in her church.

We now began to pray together. But the sister began to cry more when she heard me praying, "God, I can't help this lady. Even my faith cannot bring her a miracle." She did not know that as she cried, she brought down the altar, and as she cried more, my heart broke. I said in my heart, "This lady cannot leave this room unchanged. Something has to happen here." Then the Lord opened my eyes. I heard the Spirit of God tell her, "Go and bring your father!"

I stopped her from crying further and sat her down. I told her to bring her father the following evening since I had to stay up till that time. She said she did not have a father. I told her that was her problem. I asked her why she was bearing a compound surname. She said it was her maternal grandfather's name joined to her father's name. Her mother had never been married to her father but had jumped from one man to another. Even up till that time, the mother was still not married.

She said, "Sir, I have suffered in my life. I was a cast away and none of my uncles were willing to adopt me. They treated me like a bastard, insulting me and cursing my root. Even my own grandfather whose name I bear, sometimes tells me he wishes my mother had not brought him this shame. I became a shame and a reproach. This made me swear to take vengeance on every man I met and curse them to hell until Jesus caught up with me."

She was sobbing bitterly. I told her to wipe away her tears because her prayer was already answered.. She looked at me with amazement and said, "Sir, what do you mean?" I said, "The wild olive oil must be cut off. From today, you will have a father. From today, you will be called by a name. You will be adopted."

I told her to kneel down. As she knelt down, we began to ask God to begin to lift her from the ordinary ground and begin to graft her into the good olive tree which is contrary to nature, breaking the wildness of her oils.

As we prayed, the lady began to breathe heavily and began to behave as if she were going to faint. It was as if life was going out of her. Then, she suddenly began to tremble. As she did, glory began to come upon her life instantly. Her countenance changed and I know that the Almighty Father had, indeed, answered her prayer.

At about twelve midnight, I released her. I said, "Go. Before December, you shall become a 'Mrs' for the spirit of adoption is upon you." Today, she is married with four children.

That woman had everything she wanted in life except a covering - a husband. She had a successful business, big cars. She even sponsored big projects. But she lacked one vital thing: a husband. Men naturally felt threatened by her and got frightened at her sight - not by her money because even men who were richer than her could not stay. Some of these men were rich enough for her to live on their money all her life. Yet at the last second, they always ran away.

The president of that chapter told me how three brothers from that chapter had inexplicably broken off their engagement even though she was more beautiful than the wives they later married.

Even in matters of humility and brokenness, she was far more humble and broken than these other women. It was after they had married the other women that their follies began to dawn on them and they began to yearn for her again. The fault wasn't theirs. A curse was operating in the lady's life. Today, God shall remove from you whatever curse may be operating in your life!

If you are in this situation, your background is possibly faulty. The wild olive oil must stop hunting you. It might not be a demon at all. It could be the wild olive oil that you inherited.

The Bible says, "You were grafted contrary to nature." Today, you can ask God to take you from that limiting situation and grant you the grace to operate contrary to nature.

Perhaps, members of your family die young, with the oldest person there probably not more than 45 years old, and you are afraid you will also die young. Maybe your sisters never got married or you come from a family where first daughters never got married. Today, you can break that wild olive oil.

If you come from a background where the common problem is barrenness. Today, that wild olive oil has to cease flowing in your life. Perhaps, you took over a fight from your father - a family problem, a land or a house dispute - and today, you are the one pursuing the matter in the court. It could mean that the curse brought on your father by that fight is now transferred to your own house. You must cut off the wild olive oil.

It might be that in your family, women rule over the men. Perhaps you took a wife from a tribe of 'Amalekites:' giants who are too strong for you. They try to destroy God's oil from your life. Don't ever fight your wife. Rather fight the oil from her family that opposes your authority. Then your wife will bow in submission to you.

Wives don't fight your husband for whatever reason. Instead, fight the wild olive from his family. Until these things that undermine the word of God in people's lives are broken from them, their deliverance cannot be perfect.

You must invite by covenant today the Holy Spirit to take hold of your own olive tree and let the shake-up begin now. Let Him begin to do a cleansing work on you by Himself. Let Him trace the oil in you to your father's house, to your village, to the graveyards of your ancestors. Let Him follow you to all the lands where your forefathers have once sojourned, wherever they picked up demons while sojourning there.

Read what the Bible says:
"And they also, if they abide not still in unbelief, shall be grafted in: for God is able to graff them in again" (Romans 11:23).

Abraham suffered the repercussions of his wanderings. As he went about, he was forced to do things he naturally would not have done, and picked up demonic traits in the process. When he was in Egypt, he behaved like Egyptians telling lies contrary to his oil. This was an Egyptian spirit which he transferred to his own son Isaac who later began to tell lies too.

The condition that adversely contends with your destiny will ultimately contend with your children's destiny far more than your own if allowed to remain. That is the law we are talking about. It may as well account for why you are suffering today.

You must locate those wild olive branches. The oil of God must search them out.

It is time we declare a fast. It is time that our own gates be opened so that they can take over the oil of our land, so that we can be worthy trees before the Lord.

Jacob cheated Laban by stealing cattle from him by the 'anointing." If you are a pastor who tells lies today by the anointing, your children will become "thorns in your flesh: eventually. It is worth noting that God does not often bring out the nakedness of pastors before their congregations. He uses their family, especially the children, to torment them for their unfaithfulness. This has been the pattern even right from Bible days.

God does not defend unholy anointing. Otherwise, many people would have died. Because Jacob used his unholy anointing to cheat, God decided to punish him by allowing an unclean man to rape Dinah, his only dear daughter. The fact that his sons later killed the rapist only aggravated Jacob's sorrow.

If is doubtful if that girl ever got married again. The father, Jacob was the reason for Dinah's suffering. It was with Jacob that God had a controversy, though Dinah had to share in the punishment.

In heaven, Jacob's children would accuse him the same way he accused and cursed them. The only good one among them was Joseph. All the others were murderers, liars and robbers. They were hard working people, no doubt. But they were caught up in the web of their father's misdeeds - with his wild olive oil spreading to them like wild fire.

Jacob told an unbeliever, Pharaoh, that all his years had been short but bad. What a testimony for a great man of God! What a painful end. May that never be your end.

Howbeit ministers, you may be young now but beware of the years to come. As you walk in the present, these years might expose your frailties in the future. You must work out your own salvation with fear and trembling.

Just like I have been telling people recently, I protest the caliber of our upcoming younger ministers. They have not gone through the kind of training they need. They move too fast and have little knowledge and maturity in the work of righteousness or how to handle it. They make mistakes everywhere, displaying the nakedness of their priesthood everywhere they go. They flagrantly disobey and violate simple matters that the Scripture has settled as if they are daring God in heaven.

In a way that I have never seen any generation do before, our younger ministers get bolder by the day in disobeying God. Yet they think the anointing oil will cover them. Even when no one in their congregation dares look into their eyes, God will dare them. He is the owner of that congregation. He will defend the righteous for the sake of His name.

Since I have been raised to prepare the Church for rapture, and if, throughout my ministering here, the rapturable Church is not born, it means my ministry has not been successful no matter how many miracles and deliverances took place. The glorious Church must be born and the glorious Church is supposed to be led by a powerful, transparent priesthood, ministers, and people of high calling and integrity.

Why would a president of a nation come to my little house to ask me to pray for him? It is because he saw an anointing he never saw elsewhere. I have never had to do a press release.

No pressmen, even the born again among them who attend my meetings, are allowed to publish anything on me. I tell them that whoever publishes anything on me shall be cursed. So they do not publish anything about me. My rewarder is coming. I work in such a way that I should not be killed before my work is over.

If you have children born outside of wedlock, such children are not provided for in the covenant of God. This means they lack spiritual covering and identity. What you can do is make those children holy by releasing the spirit of adoption, calling upon the Lord to take over and clean that aspect of your unholiness.

If the first fruit is holy, the lamb is also holy. The fact that some Christians were born out of wedlock gave them a strange foundation. It also makes them unholy. You have to dig into your background to see if you were involved in abortion and fornication with all kinds of strangers to see if you had or still have family shrines.

This goes beyond yourself. Ask if your father ever got involved in any kind of iniquity, fornication and unseemliness. Perhaps, your father was involved in immoral affairs with women. That might be the reason why you are always drawn towards women. It is a wild oil heritage. Write down your father's name and all the stories you heard about him. Perhaps human blood was shed in your family or you have an herbalist in your family. All these things would make the wild olive oil still flow in the family.

Write down the details of some of your father's negative exploits. Did everybody in the village cheat him? Take note of this for the same may be coming upon you already. Some people do not know why they cannot help fornicating. It may be because their parents could not help fornicating. They too may have taken this from their own parents.

This thing flows through generations - so much that no member of the family escapes its hold. Even those that are born again still get bound by it. If the spirit of drunkenness controls you. It may be an indication that the first people who tapped palm wine in your village came from your family.

It even means that there is a covenant of palm wine tapping into your house. The law of that spirit has caught up with your throat so much that you cannot break the habit. It is a calling from the spirit of your family. Write it down.

If you do not know what your root looks like, write it down. Recall everything you can remember, and the Holy Spirit will help you along. It is also possible to inherit the wild oil by marriage.

Declare a fast. At the end of your fast, bring out the paper. After you have prayed for the destruction of the wild olive oil in your life, quote John 15:1-2 and Romans 11:16, 24. Anoint the paper with oil and say, "*God, let your own olive tree now with your own olive oil blow over these things. Let the covenant between my soul and the mystery in this paper be broken in Jesus' name.*" Then you can arise and become new.

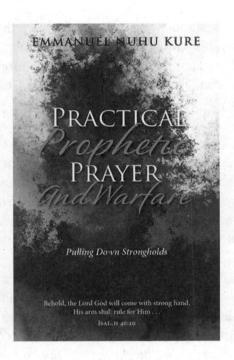

CHAPTER
6

OPEN THE GATE OF LEBANON

In Revelation 7:1-3, we are told that there are four angels in the four winds, and these four angels control the life of the whole world. Ask the angels of the four winds to open up the mystery of this land.

Call forth the spirit in the satanic world that opens up the gates, the land and the spirit of Islam. Command that spirit to open those gates for us so that we can step in and take over that which was taken captive and that which was held against us.

By taking this stand, we gain control over the life and the power in any individual that carries the unction that is oppressed by Islam and has, because of that oppression, risen to oppress and steal from us whether in or out of government. The Bible says:

"Hast thou commanded the morning since thy days; and caused the dayspring to know his place; That it might take hold of the ends of the earth, that the wicked might be shaken out of it? It is turned as clay to the seal; and they stand as a garment. And from the wicked their light is withholden, and the high arm shall be broken" (Job 38:12-15).

From this scripture we can command the cedar of the areas controlled by the forces of Islam to burn. Can you imagine telling your enemy to open his doors so that you can burn him with fire? Yet this is a prophetic command. *"Open thy door, O Lebanon, that the fire might devour thy cedars"* (Zechariah 11:1).

This means destroying the very fountain and foundation of the pillars that give him life so that by the devouring of that fire, he shall not be able to stand against you again.

Every city has doors and gates. As you wake up in the morning, ask the city where you dwell to open her doors and gates both in the physical and the spiritual realms. For strategic reasons as will be explained later, you can command the gates to open up to renew covenants for the land every Friday.

Only a few people know that covenants are renewed every seventh day. For nations, lands and cities, it is every seven years. Therefore, every seven years, demons renew covenants with different villages, towns, cities and nations.

I know of a town in Calabar (Cross River State) in Nigeria where up until now, demon worshippers go around farmlands every seventh year to renew their covenants. The elders of that land go around the city dedicating the soil unto Satan. There is a precedent in the Bible which the devil has perverted to lure people into establishing covenants that sell the land, the resources and its inhabitants to him.

"But in the seventh year shall be a Sabbath of rest unto the Lord, a Sabbath for the LORD: thou shalt neither sow thy field nor prune thy vineyard" (Leviticus 25:4).

It therefore goes without saying that every seventh day (God rested on the seventh day) is a gate. Our meetings on Sundays are gates, though many are ignorant of this. Jesus resurrected on a Sunday. Hence Sunday marks the beginning of a new week as well as the beginning of the New Testament Church.

That day the gates of heaven opened because death could not hold Jesus captive. For Islam, their gate is on Fridays. For some Eastern religions, it is Thursdays. So, if you are going to command the cedar to open, it should be on a Friday. If you are going to free yourself from every Islam influenced manipulation, it should be on a Friday. Before they call their faithful to their early morning prayer at five o'clock, raise a cry unto the Lord. You don't need to pray every day at 5 a.m. But on Fridays, command their gates and doors to open. Then command fire to devour them.

Everything we do is by the order of the Lord. As in Zechariah 11:1, we are today speaking to the north, "Open thy gates that fire may devour the pillars by which you stand, and that the Spirit of the Lord might release unto my life that which belongs to me." That is why we are making the Friday prayers permanent.

The major spirit controlling the desert is the spirit of the dead and of dryness. Of course, death means emptiness and dryness.

You will notice that in every Islamic stronghold or city you go to, the major rituals they do are with the dead. They use religion to conjure powers from the dead.

I would tell you my experience in Kano. It is not in every graveyard in Kano that you see Muslims gather. However, if you go into the real Kano city, there are particular graveyards where the biggest and the oldest mallams or great men who did a lot of rituals, are buried. You will find their people with torn pages of the Koran making incantations day and night. Right there, you will see them tear one page of the Koran and repeat that page over and over throughout the day, invoking the spirit of the dead.

These are people who get paid by some rich men to repeatedly invoke the spirit of the dead to take care of the land. That is why every operation that enters into the land has to do with the dead. There is why, if you transact business in the land, it ends up dying, it ends up being strangulated. You feel you are struggling. In fact, when you travel out of the north - Sokoto, Kano, Katsina (the core Islamic areas) - and you begin to enter Kaduna, it would look as though you are just entering civilization - as if you are just free from a tense, scorching atmosphere.

Once you begin to move from these areas down to Jos and the south, you begin to feel some air of freedom. There are Muslims in those places. But you don't feel that tension because the Muslims in those places don't, in most instances, practice fetishism like they do in those hardcore areas of the north.

Do not come to prayers as ignorant believers. Come to release the key that opens the land so that, by using that key, you can begin to breathe well. By that key, you stay in your city and sleep well.

Immediately when I arrived in Sakata during the 1998 Sakata prayer conference, one of the reports I received was that there was a place in Sakata that looked like the "Ka'aba" in Mecca where Usman Danfodio was buried along with some of the big religious leaders. If you go to the graveyard today, you will still meet men reading the Koran, calling and speaking to the spirits of the dead.

You should command the door of the city to open on Friday because it is the day they make the official sacrifice. That is the day the "Sabbath" is kept. That is the day the doors, the mysteries and the customs that rule the lives of the people open up. Why? To renew with them the covenant of life or the oppression of the outsiders who don't belong to that culture. Their inability to prosper in the land is renewed at the opening of each Friday.

Therefore, when the gate closes in the evening, it means that, for another seven days, the struggle of the non-indigent or the non-Muslim is sealed. He cannot stand where his peers stand even if he is an indigent because the gate does not recognize him since he did not make a sacrifice to it.

The only thing he can do is stand when the gate is opening. That was what Elisha took advantage of when he said *"If thou see me when I am taken from thee, it shall be so unto thee"* (2 Kings 2:10b).
It is when the gate is opened that you will come forth to pass your decree. Then life will be released unto you. However, when you miss the gate and you go about trying to break down

the walls after the gate has been closed, you will not succeed. Elisha was there when Elijah was taken and Elisha got a double anointing.

In the New Testament, the Bible say that each time they stirred the waters, the first person that jumped into the water got his healing.

"Now there is at Jerusalem by the sheep market a pool, which is called in the Hebrew tongue Bethesda, having five porches. In these lay a great multitude of impotent folk, of blind, halt, withered, waiting for the moving of the water. For an angel went down at a certain season into the pool, and troubled the water: whosoever then first after the troubling of the water stepped in was made whole of whatsoever disease he had" (John 2:2-4).

The gate of the finger of the power of God was opened with the stirring of the waters. And because they jumped in, they got their healing. You will command the gate to open. It recognizes those covenant words because Friday is a covenant day for every Islamic city in the Islamic world. It is the day when the lives of the indigents of those cities are renewed. It is the day you should step into those gates and command the pillars that are the shadows of death. You should command the covenant, the spirit of death, to break out from people's lives.

The Bible says that in the ages to come, He might show us the hidden riches. That is what God is showing us now. It is when you are able to catch the hidden riches that the treasures of darkness can be transferred to you for you to become bigger than the men of darkness. Until you have the principles by which they exist and know how to speak unto them, you will not be able to prevail against them.

As long as you live in any of the Islamic cities, you will want to breathe well. If you want to remain alive when they stage their riots, you must understand this secret. Likewise, as long as you are a businessman and you desire to get oil from the government or the people of any Islamic city, you must understand this mystery. As long as you want to prosper in the city, to build for yourself rivers that will keep you alive, you must understand this mystery.

As long as you operate by this principle, those who could not build houses will begin to build. Those who have no cars will own cars because the land will begin to loosen up and say, "Oppress everybody, minus him." And the gate will say, "Yes, I have a covenant of life with you" and it will not allow death to devour you or your business.

That is the mystery of every seven days. Every seven years there is a renewal of covenant for lands. Every 49 years (seven years times seven) there is a renewal of covenant, not just for land but for a generation. And the calling forth of a new destiny. That is how those years operate.

That is the mystery by which our lives operate every year. And that is why the Bible declares the fiftieth year as the year of liberty.

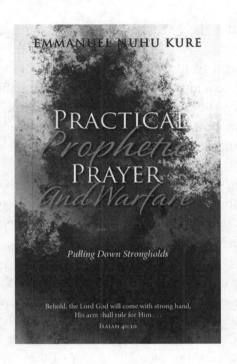

CHAPTER
7

ALTARS AND THRONES
ARE ESTABLISHED
BY ORDINANCES

FIRSTLY, **I AM** going to introduce you to the rudiments of setting up thrones and how to set up your own thrones. The battle of thrones is a daily reality of life that we cannot shy away from. Therefore, I am going to teach you how to set up a throne that is the Throne of God over your life.

Whenever you go to war and the Throne of God is not seated over you, you cannot win because it is a battle of thrones. So, whenever your enemy comes against you, he brings his thrones with him, his authority and his gods carrying them into your house to wage war against you.

I am starting on a rhythm of war. I am going to set up thrones against thrones. I am going to teach you how to set up thrones so that when you go to war, you won't look back or retreat but advance to victory.

Thrones are established by ordinances. When the Lord makes a vow, He says, "I vow by myself and my word shall not return unto me void ... that unto me every knee shall bow!" God said, "I have vowed unto David my servant that I shall not cast his children from my face." Because of that vow, the sons of David were secure in the day of iniquity.

"Can wicked rulers be allied with you, those who frame injustice by statute? They band together against the life of the righteous and condemn the innocent to death. But the Lord has become my stronghold, and my God the rock of my refuge. He will bring back on them their iniquity and wipe them out for their wickedness; the Lord our God will wipe them out" (Psalm 94:20-23).

In verse 20, we can see clearly that it is by decree that the Lord frames mischief against your enemies. All He does is pass a decree over you, and your situation will change.

Governments, especially military ones, rule by decrees which are non-negotiable. Heaven does not operate by democracy but by supreme laws. No one questions the laws of God which are absolute. You don't negotiate them. You either live by them and receive His blessings or live outside them and be at the mercy of Satan.

Beloved, I want to tell you every son of perdition that boasts against you possibly has a throne of iniquity sitting over him as his defence and confidence. It may not be an attacking demon. Because he understands the strength of his position in the spirit and knows what influence he wields in the society, he confidently turns the whole of that power and demonic machinery against your life.

It is still the throne of iniquity speaking against you. You can smash it down. If the man is privileged to occupy a vantage position over you and takes advantage of that to oppress you, the Lord has an answer for him.

When an unbeliever who wallows in iniquity has the guts to boast against you, it is a clear indication that a throne of iniquity is speaking against your life and destiny. It is your business to fire back at it.

When God was telling Amos to go to war, He instructed him to "*Smite the lintel of the door...*" for in the lintel of the door lies the symbol of the covenant of the life of that person. The lintel of the door carries the secret of the house.

"*I saw the Lord standing beside the altar, and he said: 'Strike the capitals until the thresholds shake, and shatter them on the heads of all the people; and those who are left of them I will kill with the sword; not one of them shall flee away; not one of them shall escape'*" (Amos 9:1).

"*I saw the Lord standing...*" not sitting. When the Lord stands, it means He is supervising judgment. It might be for good or evil. But He is supervising judgment all the same. Jesus stands over the altar as our High Priest. The Bible says He stands and still makes intercession for our lives.

"Consequently, he is able to save to the uttermost those who draw near to God through him, since he always lives to make intercession for them" (Hebrews 7:25).

When the throne of iniquity speaks and boasts against you through the sons of disobedience, the Lord does not sit down to defend you. Rather, He stands on the altar. Do you know why? It is the altar that vomits the fire for the Lord to answer by fire.

"Be sober-minded; be watchful. Your adversary the devil prowls around like a roaring lion, seeking someone to devour " (1 Peter 5:8).

How then can we get these thrones to speak for us? How do we build an altar?

If a sorcerer or a "juju man" goes to invoke his demons from the bush and make his concoctions to attack you will all the powers of hell and their mandate on his head, the questions is, at such times, what do you do.?

He probably will be waiting for you to confront him with what you claim to have. If, at that time, you have nothing to disarm and deal with him, may God have mercy on you. One of the worst things that can happen in the life of any child of God is, after boasting of the power of the Lord and serving God for many years, for the enemy to catch him unguarded.

The enemy will reduce him to nothing and avenge all the years he has suffered defeat. There are some of us whom the enemy will not spare if he ever has the opportunity to deal with us. May that opportunity never come in Jesus' Name. Amen! He has heard our testimonies and he is seeking with rage to get at us.

Your God must be there always to answer the enemy as the Bible assures us. Your part is to arise and serve God from the position of brokenness. Whoever serves God from that position of brokenness is conscious of his infirmities and limitations.

HOW TO RAISE ALTARS

How do I raise an altar? You cannot raise an altar until you understand the spiritual connection between altars and ordinances. And you cannot understand ordinances if you don't know how to build an altar. Altars sustain ordinances. It is when you have an altar over your life that the altar carries out the ordinances that come out of your mouth.

Many of us call ourselves kings and priests without knowing how to rule and officiate as priests. I want to say clearly that when you speak with your authority as a child of God, through your positive confessions, it is your altar that carries it through.

You, as a king, speak from your throne to the throne of grace, and minister as a priest from your altar to the Lamb's altar in heaven from where you draw power. That is the power behind your power. It is the invisible altar with invisible spirits (angels) around you.

When you build an altar, it becomes like the chariot that carried the law in Ezekiel chapter one from which the Lord speaks.
.
We notice in the Bible that any battle to which the children of

Israel carried the Ark of the Lord they won. Any battle they failed to take the Ark of the Lord, they suffered defeat.

Do you know that your soul has an altar inside, a place of sacrifice where you make contact with God? You are a temple and also the priest of that temple. Do you realize that behind your physical temple there must necessarily be within you a spiritual altar?

So, when situations come against you with the mandate of hell and all the powers of Satan seated on top of it, they crumble and bow when they see the Lord seated upon your head in power.

Each time Isaiah said he saw the Lord seated upon His throne, he meant that the Lord was alive unto His responsibilities in his own life because of his righteousness on earth. That is why the Bible says Jesus is still daily making intercession for us. However, you need to bring Jesus to work over your situation in battle. From today, begin to bring your feet down to possess the goodness of the Lord in the :Garden of Eden."

In these last days, one of the things that will give you joy and comfort is the release of your soul. Everything that obstructs your soul, be it from the food you eat to sickness, etc., should be broken so that you can have peace flowing with God.

It is much better to fight with the enemy without that the enemy within. The enemy within is sometimes stronger and more resilient that the enemy without. You must destroy the enemy within. Just set the throne of God to purge it out.

HOW IS AN ALTAR BUILT?
Altars are built by making covenants.

"Come, everyone who thirsts, come to the waters; and he who has no money, come, buy and eat! Come, buy wine and milk without money and without price. Why do you spend your money for that which is not bread, and your labor for that which does not satisfy? Listen diligently to me, and eat what is good, and delight yourselves in rich food. Incline your ear, and come to me; hear, that your soul may live; and I will make with you an everlasting covenant, my steadfast, sure love for David. Behold, I made him a witness to the peoples, a leader and commander for the peoples. Behold, you shall call a nation that you do not know, and a nation that did not know you shall run to you, because of the Lord your God, and of the Holy One of Israel, for he has glorified you" (Isaiah 55:1-5).

Altars call men to serve you. When you set an altar, it makes people who know you to bless you. It attracts by the power of God. It becomes your medicine, the magnet that calls people to you, the magnet that manifests and establishes your favor.

How do you build an altar? It is by making a covenant. But how do you get to the covenant stage?

1. THROUGH WORSHIP: The day you want to build an altar, start by stepping into God's presence and acknowledge Him and what He is to you, your environment, to people and to the nations.

How do you worship? Worship is the sense of acknowledging and appreciating God's might. I do not mean just coming before the Lord to sing praises, but the specific things you need to do when you are building an altar unto the Lord.

You should acknowledge His Lordship, His Person, who He is and what He is to you as an individual, to your environment, your nation, your fellow human beings as well as to the demons. When you acknowledge that, you are making God spread His arms over you. You will say, "My Father, You are the ruler of the heavens and the earth. You are all that I know. You are my God. In Your presence, I lose my relevance. You are my relevance."

When you start acknowledging God at this level, you are stirring Him up to arise on your behalf to say, "Even if I have a quarrel with this man, I am not giving him over to his enemy. I am his only help. Let Me draw closer to hear what he has to say."

As you do that, acknowledge also your nothingness. It is not negative confession to tell God that He is your medicine, that you are nothing but a mere carrier of everything that He gives you.

For ministers, that is the secret of asking for more anointing. Tell Him, "God, the people are hungry and demanding more from You every day and I have nothing more to give." Ask Him to refill you. Acknowledge who you are. Acknowledge what you are and tell Him you don't want to walk on your own. You want to walk as a living altar. Before you know it, the oil of that altar will begin to pour out inside of you. When you rise to face the people, they will know God has come among them.

The Lord told me that we have not seen anything yet about miracles and that very soon the kind of miracles we will see will frighten men. Buildings will fall at the voices of some men. Thunders will come out from heaven and destroy places at the voices of others. Men will walk among people and the lame will be jumping up from the congregation and walking all over the place.

There is an anointing I am waiting for, my brethren, which is about to be released unto our generation. It is the anointing that will change the definition of the "fear of God" in the hearts of men. Men will not just fear, they will tremble and the Lord is going to use you as the first fruit of those examples. Nevertheless, the first thing is to acknowledge who you are, what you are, your place in His presence, and He will begin to change your destiny.

Every witness of God is supposed to be an olive tree. In Revelation 11, when Jesus said, "You shall be my witness," He meant you shall be His olive tree - olive oils. When you touch anything, it is His oil that touches that thing. This is what it means to be a witness.

"But you will receive power when the Holy Spirit has come upon you, and you will be my witnesses in Jerusalem and in all Judea and Samaria, and to the end of the earth" (Acts 1:8).

The oil establishes a disciple. It is the confidence that you have in God that makes you witness for Him. It is the oil that brings that confidence - the altar over your life.

If you look at the Scripture carefully, the days will come when the Church will become invincible and untouchable. The world will stand still in awe. We are entering into those days because the transformation that brings about those days is here now.

The situation that will force the Church to begin to hunger and seek God as never before is here now. The twenty-first century Church is not going to be a powerless Church. It is going to be a powerful Church as prophesied. For the kingdom of God is not in word but in power.

"Behold, you shall call a nation that you do not know, and a nation that did not know you shall run to you, because of the Lord your God, and of the Holy One of Israel, for he has glorified you" (Isaiah 55:5).

So, how do you build an altar? Acknowledge the God of the heavens and the earth, and acknowledge who you are. Refine the positions you see. A covenant is an agreement between two or more parties. You have to accept your weak position if you are the lesser party and also the stronger position of the other party. That is how you Sign a covenant, an agreement of a contract.

When you build an altar with God, you must agree that the altar will carry you because you cannot carry yourself. Spiritually, that places the altar above you. That is the reason for acknowledgement. State the position of the two of you. One is the Ruler, Lord and God. The other one is the beneficiary, the one who lives by the grace of the other.

One seeks the favor of the other and is carried by that one. The day He breaks the covenant, reproach will not only come to him, it will come to God too. For it is by you that His Name is reproached or glorified on earth. God will not break His altar in your life. God is raising nations from you, a nation that knows what He is doing.

2. THROUGH REPENTANCE: If you need a pattern from raising the altar, two major characters exemplify it.

The first example is found in Nehemiah. There you will see how he acknowledged the God of heaven when he went down on his face and humbled his heart in repentance. He knew he and his people were in trouble and were helpless.

When he heard the news of the ruins, he had to raise a cry to heaven. He had a place with God. But here was a problem. So he fell down before God in absolute brokenness and contrition.

"As soon as I heard these words I sat down and wept and mourned for days, and I continued fasting and praying before the God of heaven. And I said, "O Lord God of heaven, the great and awesome God who keeps covenant and steadfast love with those who love him and keep his commandments" (Nehemiah 1:4-5).

I am teaching you how to become invincible, how you can become the man that carries an altar. When you are doing this, please forget about your status and become like a little child before God. It you have a mat, put it beside your bed on the ground and sit down on it before God and say, "The Rock that never fails, let me hide in You. For in You is power."

If you sincerely do this with your whole heart, I assure you, this will cause a riot in heaven because God has seen you humble yourself as you sit on the ground. You do not build an altar over your life standing irreverently and just speaking in tongues as if you are talking to your fellow man. That shows you are still very strong on your feet and do not need a "physician" yet.

The prophet Ezekiel makes the second example. He was lifted up from the ground and became a walking altar. He said when he saw the Lord, his knees became weak and he fell on the ground.

"Such was the appearance of the likeness of the glory of the Lord. And when I saw it, I fell on my face, and I heard the voice of one speaking" (Ezekiel 1:28b).

You should lie down on the ground to build an altar. If you do that, no matter who you are, rich or poor, the Lord will lift you up. Get yourself some quietness. Lock yourself behind a door or get into a distant bush where nobody can see you. If you have a house under construction, please go and add one more level. Build a tower where you will live on top.

The prophets lived high up in the towers from where they watched the cities and destroyed their enemies. Elijah lived inside a tower. I follow biblical patterns in setting things. Your tower is God's physical symbol of covenant between your house and yourself.

Make your tower God's personal covenant with your family. Do not do any other thing there than pray. It is not your official chapel for the family's house. You can still keep your chapel downstairs or wherever. But that one is your "medicine." Designate it as your "Holy of Holies" into which you step when you know you must establish a covenant.

What do you do after that? Go into repentance after you have acknowledged who you are, your brokenness, how you cannot survive without Him. Tell God how, by your word, you muddled up things because you were careless with your mouth. Tell Him the truth. In some circumstances it is only one party who is guilty. Sometimes you too contribute a little to the crisis situation.

Repent! It is not a virtue to start recounting your righteousness before God when you are supposed to be in sack cloths and ashes mourning and repenting. Some of us are like that. We tell God to see good reasons why He must overlook some things and still do us good. Please, God knows all the righteous things you have done. But you must let Him know that He is indispensable and that His laws cannot be compromised.

You are not above His Laws. In this way, it means you are not insulting His integrity. Rather you respect and honor the integrity of His word. Repent completely in sackcloth and ashes, and beg Him for forgiveness. Then you will be building an altar.

Repent until you are convinced in the spirit that God has forgiven you for what you did. If there is need of restitution to be added to that repentance, vow to Him that you are going to make it and pay back. You must take steps to keep your vows. Remember, the tax collector, Zacchaeus, who upon meeting Jesus, vowed to pay four times whatever he had taken from anyone.

3. THROUGH COVENANT MAKING: It is after repentance that you start the real covenant making. At this point, you tell God exactly what you want: your supplication.

When you start the covenant agreement, bring in the provision of His Word concerning that thing. Here, you will notice that, at the altar, there is a place where the testimony was kept open. There, as you lay your request, you must also bring the provision from the Bible to back it up.

You must have studied the Scriptures relevant to your request before you bring them to God. When you bring them before Him, you must acknowledge His ability to do it. After doing this, you will call upon the Lord to arise and let His enemies be scattered. You will thereafter tell Him to raise a standard.

4. CONCLUDING THE ALTAR: You now take a gift to the Lord. Only you and the Lord know why you are giving. Where He leads you to share with the pastor so that he agrees with you, go ahead and do it. Where he does not, keep quiet.

The Spirit behind the altar you have built will follow you. Because this is a special gift, you will not put it in the normal offering. You will give it to cover a peculiar project either within the church or outside.

King David gives us an example in the Bible: *"And David built there an altar to the Lord and offered burnt offerings and peace offerings. So the Lord responded to the plea for the land, and the plague was averted from Israel"* (2 Samuel 24:25).

Peculiar offerings are given to meet peculiar needs. You will send it to where God has need for t. This is how you set the altar that sits higher than you, so that when you go speaking outside, the oil of the altar will keep softening the situation.

When you go to offer your gifts, do it with thanksgiving in your heart. Rejoice over your victory. Take a dance around your gift, not in front of your pastor, but before the Lord. It is a fellowship. Sometimes, it looks like madness, but do it. Rejoice in your spirit. That makes the Spirit of God come alive around that environment. From that day, woe betides the man that touches you because fire is raised to stand on your head and to establish that which you prayed for.

You must do something that will make God stand up to say, *"My son, come to me. Whosoever touches you, I will dismantle this day."*

When you are making that covenant, set God's face against the throne of iniquity. As you lay the real matter before God in conclusion, tell Him what you want Him to do with it. Make a demand that, from today, your words shall be prophetic words that will take hold of whatever you direct it to.

After you have finished the covenant, arise from your position and begin to thank God. Praise God, honoring His word and His Name.

5. PROPHESY TO THE SITUATION: This is when you now start speaking like a man of authority because it is your turn to speak. Sin no longer condemns you. You have already invoked the attention of heaven and the mercy of God. At that hour, nothing stands against you anymore. Arise and prophesy.

Building an altar is incomplete without prophesy. You must prophesy. Speak to the situation. Tell the situation to hear the voice of the Lord, not your voice anymore.

In the book of John 5:25, the Bible say, "*The hour comes when the dead will hear the voice of the Son of God and they that hear shall live.*" That situation that has risen up against you can be likened to death. Therefore, arise and prophesy. It shall hear the voice of the word of God through your mouth, and your situation in life shall begin to live again. The evil situation around you shall be reversed.

Please, without the prophetic note in it, your altar is incomplete. It is the prophetic move that gives it oil and empowers the altar to speak because you have already established the provision of heaven in it.

The word of God is the key of heaven. When you prophesy, doors begin to open. It is what you are prophesying that the Lord will use to dismantle the other altars. Henceforth, they cannot stand against you.

After you have finished all the prayers, you can begin to carry out what we call "prophetic action" to break the walls that had hitherto been insurmountable. What I have just taught you is actually the center point of Christian fellowship with the Lord, especially where it has to do with establishing God's authority over situations.

Once you have built an altar, your business is to set your face against those negative situations that confront you. They must die because you are now empowered by the righteousness that God has given you. This gives you the right standing to face them squarely because, from that altar, you have been legally empowered by the Lord to deal with them and all their legalities over your life.

Actually, you don't boldly confront those situations until you have built an altar. It is then that you can set your face continually against them until they are absolutely routed out, never to stand again.

You can build an altar as many times as there are problems or as many times as there are things to praise God for. You can build an altar of praise. You can build an altar of divine health and you can renew it from time to time. You can build an altar of fellowship around your house so that when people enter your home, they feel a clean atmosphere as if angels are singing.

The Bible says there are the set thrones of David. Each throne has a different meaning. You will notice that the Bible says, "The throne of iniquity shall not stand against you." The devil has different thrones for different purposes. Heaven also has different thrones for different purposes and some are established for spiritual warfare.

There are extra things you may need to add to that altar according to the kind of altar you are building. It is with the altar that the throne of God is set in your life and the covenant of the Lord is established.

Altars, covenants and thrones flow into one another. I repeat: altars, covenants and thrones flow together. There cannot be one without the others. It is the throne that establishes the covenant. As a result, they flow together. Spiritually, they are interrelated in operation.

If the altar you are building is over your family, you must bring out the words that were spoken at the dedication of Solomon's temple: "Lord, when pestilence comes upon the land and every house is affected, and there is no way or doors of escape, my house shall escape it. You shall pass over this house.

Let your Spirit sprinkle the blood of Jesus over my house - it shall pass over. Lord, in the day of turmoil, with killings and blood-letting everywhere, even if my office is on fire, you will take me in the chariot that took Philip, and I shall not be found in the fire. Neither shall my children be found in the fire. So let it be established for my family today in the Name of Jesus."

That establishes an altar. By this you are setting a cover of fellowship, oil that will cover your house for life. It shall be a part of the covenant-speaking Solomon's prayer of agreement.

You don't build altars only when there are troubles. You build altars of protection when there is no trouble at all so that in the day of trouble, it will preserve you.

I pray often for my children. I say, "God, even when I sin, my children shall not lack heritage, for your covenant is from everlasting to everlasting. You will not cut me off and hand me over to my enemies who have waited to see my fall. In the day I fall, they will pick up the pieces and tear me apart. In that day, hide me from their eyes. Let my judgment be of you and of you alone."

Every man who carries oil must learn how to establish this kind of covenant. It is then he can live an invisible life. Above all, do you know that altars control the day and the night? According to the book of Peter, "The earth exists by the word of the Lord, by the word of the Lord the heavens were made."

There are different levels of altars. When you are building more serious altars, you must make more serious sacrifices. Some problems require you to fast for one day while others require that you fast for three of more days.

Do you know that by an altar, David held at bay the power of darkness, and stopped the evil kingdom from smiting him? You can stop Nigeria or whichever country you live in from stealing from you. You can stop the situation in your office, home, business, etc., from destroying your life. You can open a doorway where there was none before.

Do you know that it is by the ordinances flowing from this covenant that the heavens are commanded to relate to you? The stars, the moon and the sun are controlled by the ordinances of heaven.

The golden altar in heaven establishes God's ordinances on earth. When He says, "Touch not," it is the altar that executes His commands. Therefore, whoever disobeys the ordinances of "Touch not," the altar will release fire to burn him.

When you are establishing an altar to deal with a situation and God says, "Touch not" but the situation insists on touching you, the altar will release a fire to burn it. You will discover that God will amazingly raise a favorable situation to counter those negative circumstances that are bent on overwhelming you.

Amazingly, to the glory of God, this is what has always happened in my life. When somebody says, "I will deal with you" and gives a deadline when the deadline expires, the Lord would deal with them.

The Bible says:
"Thus says the Lord, who gives the sun for light by day and the fixed order of the moon and the stars for light by night, who stirs up the sea so that its waves roar— the Lord of hosts is his name: "If this fixed order departs from before me, declares the Lord, then shall the offspring of Israel cease from being a nation before me forever" (Jeremiah 31:35-36).

There is a spiritual law that controls the sun, the moon and the stars. It was ordained in them by God. This law is the operating manual for the sun, moon and the stars. It is called the ordinances. When the Lord says, *"The sun shall not smite you by day nor the moon by night,"* what actually shields you from being smitten are ordinances.

Nevertheless, these ordinances are to be projected into these heavenly bodies (the sun, moon and stars) by you, enforcing what God has commanded them to do on your behalf. When God created the heavens and the earth, the earth was supposed to accommodate and shield your life, not destroy it.

Therefore, when men manipulate it to destroy you, you can command the earth to only respond to the former agreement with God which is to keep you alive. The Bible says in Psalm 8:6 that God has given us dominion over all the works of His hand. What a privilege!

Chapter Seven

It is by ordinances that your life is kept. Ordinances can stop the devil from eating up your life. In the day when the waster descended to waste David, a devourer was sent to kill the whole of Israel. But when David built an altar and made an offering, the plague was stopped.

"And David built there an altar to the Lord and presented burnt offerings and peace offerings and called on the Lord, and the Lord answered him with fire from heaven upon the altar of burnt offering. Then the Lord commanded the angel, and he put his sword back into its sheath" (1Chronicles 21:26-27).

The ordinances of David's sacrifice constituted a spiritual legislation that ascended to God in Heaven and descended on the devourer on earth. This exercise held back the devourer from destroying the place where David was making the offering.

David would have died that day in that instance. Today, the situation that has been smiting you shall smite you no more. I want you to bear in mind that there are ordinances that control human behavior and the elements. They determine what they do. You can contribute to the ordinance when you are making your covenant.

In the Bible, Jeremiah 31:35 specifically refers to ordinances "which divided the sea ... when the waves thereof roar ..." Today, when the waves roar against you, the Spirit of the Lord will divide them and take them away from you. That is what this Bible passage means.

When the Lord used the word "need" in verse 36 of Jeremiah 31, it is the word of covenant. The seed of Israel has to do with the seed of Jesse which is Jesus Christ. From now on, any astrologer or sorcerer that manipulates the sun against you, the sun shall smite him. From today, the moon shall smite anybody who seeks to rob you of sleep in the night and manilulates it against .you. Reverse the ordinances in the heavenly places, and their decree will be reversed.

It is by ordinances that these heavenly powers rule. They that manipulate the environment against you go around the city evenings to release their spell into the atmosphere. You can also reverse their authority in the atmosphere by ordinances. From today, your battles are won.

According to the book of Isaiah, the Lord causes trouble for our enemies. He makes the wave of trouble to pass across the nations in the evenings. Clearly, the Lord rises upon the wings of trouble:

"The nations roar like the roaring of many waters, but he will rebuke them, and they will flee far away, chased like chaff on the mountains before the wind and whirling dust before the storm. At evening time, behold, terror! Before morning, they are no more! This is the portion of those who loot us, and the lot of those who plunder us" (Isaiah 17:13-14).

The evening time (4:00 to 7:00 pm) is so strategic for God to cause trouble for human beings. At such times, the Lord comes out to watch over His children to avenge any wickedness against them. That is also the time He descends to have fellowship with them.

The best time to make prophetic declarations is in the early hours of the morning. You can call forth before the rising of the sun and make the day spring to carry it out according to Job:

"Have you commanded the morning since your days began,

and caused the dawn to know its place, that it might take hold of the skirts of the earth, and the wicked be shaken out of it? (Job 38:12-13)

Do you know that God sits over the night and causes it to give birth to His revelation in your life? And He sits over the morning to make it give birth to a fresh, beautiful you? I want you to understand that there are ordinances that force the earth to ensure that you have a pleasant morning and blessed evening.

Therefore, woe betide that element that may attempt to break those ordinances. If you understand and walk by this revelation, there will be divine productivity in everything you do in life. I guarantee you, anything you touch will be fruitful.

The day the Lord said, "Let there be light," there was light, and the Lord called the light "day, and called the darkness "night." He commanded the day to recognize your birth, and not to steal anything from your life.

God had to take Jeremiah back to that level when He said: *"Thus says the Lord: If you can break my covenant with the day and my covenant with the night, so that day and night will not come at their appointed time, then also my covenant with David my servant may be broken, so that he shall not have a son to reign on his throne, and my covenant with the Levitical priests my ministers. As the host of heaven cannot be numbered and the sands of the sea cannot be measured, so I will multiply the offspring of David my servant, and the Levitical priests who minister to me"* (Jeremiah 33:20-22).

You will give birth to a kindred of rulers. This is going to be your portion henceforth. "...And with the Levite ... ministers." Do you remember that Jesus said He made you kings and priests? Are you therefore, a Levite or His ministers?

God has a covenant to defend His ministers, a covenant to defend the sons of David and the lion of the tribe of Judah. The root of Jesse has begotten us unto himself. As David was, so are we. Every covenant that was with David came unto us. It is the same law that establishes out lives and our fellowship in the Lord Jesus.

Do you know what that means? It means, in material possession, in power and in number, He will multiply the seed of David. However, please note, "...*and the Levites and minister unto me...*" Is your life still ministering to God? If yes, you are qualified. If your life has stopped ministering to God, you are disqualified.

Let that not depart from you. God said, "If my covenant be not with day and night, and if I have not appointed the ordinances of heaven and earth, then can your life be wasted. However, if I have appointed the ordinances in heaven, curse betides the situation that wants to cast away your life." That is the vow God is putting up here.

Call upon the Lord that, from today, the day must recognize you. From today, the Lord will institute and reestablish the power of the covenant. He established by day. Reestablish it again with the night for your life. This will activate the mystery of the day that will give you your portion.

Curse betide that mystery that makes your portion to be reversed, reduced or not add up to you according to the proportion of your work. From today, you will ask God to purge out these mysteries in the day that resists the works of your hand. Tell the covenant to smite that thing.

God intends His covenant to protect you. Therefore, there is protection for you day and night. What I am asking you to do is invoke that protection to begin to speak on your behalf. By ordinances, your life exists. By ordinances, your business exists. Even your breath is controlled by ordinances. Both day and night must not destroy your business.

Tell God to purge every strange ordinance that has been released in the air and mixed with the sun, the moon and the stars against you. From today, they shall not control your life anymore. If you are steadily losing your sanity or feeling bodily discomfort, or are troubled by one health problem or the other, ask God by the covenant of day and night to purge it out of your life. Arise and break that cycle of sickness and disease, they will not stand against your life again. Call upon the Lord to begin to lift away the face of poverty that has always humiliated you.

According to the ordinances of heaven, a servant shall not serve forever. For every servant, there is a year of liberty. Even in the days of the children of Israel, slaves were set free after some years as slaves because by the ordinance of God, one day a slave will become a master. Check your scriptures very well to see that slaves don't stay forever in Israel. There is a year of liberty, except where the servant decides to remain with the master by choice.

"You shall thus consecrate the fiftieth year and proclaim release though the land to all its inhabitants. It shall be jubilee for you, and each of you shall return to his own property, and each of you shall return to his family" (Leviticus 25:10 NAS).

Your slavery shall be broken. Everyone who serves others will be served one day. A say when you too shall become a master of a multitude, whereupon you will only refer to the master you served as mentor.

You will keep good relations with him. There is an ordinance for everyone. Hence, I said even if you are the poorest of men, God has the day of liberty from your poverty.

The mystery that puts an end to your days of servitude is the mystery of day and night because your years are numbered by day and night. With every day you grow older - with everyday your years are counted. There is a day you will wake up to be a free man forever.

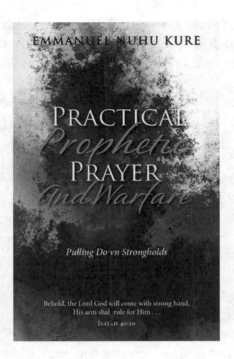

CHAPTER
8

ORDINANCES
CONTROL LIFE

IN MOST CASES, when men rise up to prophesy, they speak with fervency from the earth, and send the words into the heavens expecting the words to control affairs on earth. From today, we shall send down the words into the heavens expecting the words to control affairs on earth. From today, we shall send down the words from the heavens and the heavens shall take hold of the earth and rule for us.

"And in that day I will answer, declares the Lord, I will answer the heavens, and they shall answer the earth" (Hosea 2:21).

The prophetic unction works from the heavens to the earth. It does not work from the earth to heaven. I shall explain this so that you will leave your present state and make your permanent abode in the heavens. From there, you can reign over the earth. From there, you can reign over your enemies.

Henceforth, your enemies shall not escape your sword. Everything you say shall be binding on them. Your friends will not escape you. Every blessing you speak unto them shall follow them. You shall begin to function as a priest. Everyone that accepts Jesus as Lord and Savior has been made a priest in the order of Melchizedek by His death and resurrection.

That is why the Bible says in Revelation 1:6 that we have been made kings and priests:

"And made us a kingdom, priests to his God and Father, to him be glory and dominion forever and ever. Amen" (Revelation 1:6).

I want you to understand that prophesy originates from the heavens. It is not a product of the earth. The man that prophesies must call upon the heavens to do what he wants done. Without this, there will be no stamp of authority to perform the words he has declared.

For instance, if you want to curse or bless somebody, tell the fellow, "The heavens curse or bless you," and that settles it.

You speak as a priest commanding the heavens to carry out your instructions, and the heavens oblige.

ORDINANCES FROM HEAVEN

The heavens are actually the dwelling place of the ordinances that control the earth. God deposited in heaven these laws that cause the sun, the moon and the stars to release life to us and to nature. They cause the ground to open up and yield its fruit. The law that governs the earth is from the heavens.

Therefore, if you want to ultimately control the power that exists on earth, you have to control it from the heavens. When I am talking about the heavens, I am not talking about the throne where God dwells. God dwells in the heaven of heavens. I am talking about where the firmaments are, where the waters on earth were folded.

The Bible says:
"In the beginning, God created the heavens and the earth. The earth was without form and void, and darkness was over the face of the deep. And the Spirit of God was hovering over the face of the waters" (Genesis 1:1-2).

If you read further, you will see that God divided the waters and called the firmament heaven. The realm of the waters - heavens above the clouds is where these metaphysical laws that control the earth exist. That is why the Spirit of the Lord still dwells there, in the deep. That is what Amos tells us. If you look at Amos chapter 5, you will find out that the Spirit of the Lord dwells in the seven stars in the realms of the heavens.

What this means is that the water of the sea must be above the earth to be poured on the face of the earth from the heavens. This is because the word by which the earth exists was declared by the Spirit of the Lord that moved in the deep and the

Lord said, "Let there be ..." In Peter, the Bible says the earth is sustained by that word, meaning that those ordinances that control the day and night exist inside the heavens where the Lord God Himself is the power. He is the power that moves it, just as prophet Amos tells us:

"He who made the Pleiades and Orion, and turns deep darkness into the morning and darkens the day into night, who calls for the waters of the sea and pours them out on the surface of the earth, the Lord is his name " (Amos 5:8).

I am taking you into secrets not meant for children. They are meant for serious and mature Christians who ae ready to take their destinies in their hands and align it with God and the Holy Spirit. From today, your destiny will do God's will but you must be ready to be part and parcel of the work of creation.

THE HEAVEN RULES

In Daniel 4:26, the Bible says, *"And as it was commanded to leave the stump of the roots of the tree, your kingdom shall be confirmed for you from the time that you know that Heaven rules."*

The powers of the heavens are the powers that control the ordinances of the earth. That is why it says when you curse, let the heavens curse. Otherwise, the curse is powerless and ineffective. When you bless, let the heavens bless. Otherwise, your blessing is useless.

The real force that controls the earth comes from that place called the heavens. The heavens are the place above the firmament in the heavens. That is where these ordinances operate. There are no ordinances in heaven where God rules. There is no day or night there. You will discover that the ordinances will end with the coming of the Lord Jesus Christ.

In Matthew 24, the Bible says the powers of the heavens will be shaken. When referring to the last days in Haggai, God says, "And I will shake the heavens and I will shake the earth." When the Lord begins to shake the heavens, it means He is reshuffling the decrees by which the earth operates. It means the earth is about to take a new shape.

When Jesus comes, the decrees that control the earth will be reshuffled. That is why I am sure about your anointing, about the quality of the things you are to carry in this end time. There is going to be a reshuffling of anointing. This is the Spirit of prophesy, the revelation of God, the mind of God.

"Immediately after the tribulation of those days the sun will be darkened, and the moon will not give its light, and the stars will fall from heaven, and the powers of the heavens will be shaken"(Matthew 24:29).

It is against the law of God for the sun and the moon to darken. They are supposed to appear by day and by night respectively, giving light.

One of the greatest forces that herbalists use against people is the star. They believe that star represents man and his destiny, which is true. This means they understand the laws and dynamics of astrology.

When Jesus was born, wise men from the East came to worship Him. They said they had seen His star in the East. As astrologers, they could read the information in the star of Jesus and the location of His birth, just as they said, *"Where is He who has been born King of the Jews? For we have seen His star in the East and have come to worship Him"* (Matthew 2:2

NKJV).

The star by itself is a cauldron. By speaking into the stars, they can manipulate you to carry out whatever they want you to do. When the Bible says the stars will fall, it means that the powers of the herbalists and Satan shall be broken. The controlling power in hell shall be broken, meaning that even the laws of hell shall be destroyed. The ordinances of darkness shall stand powerless in that day.

The Bible says, *"And the stars shall fall from heaven and powers of the heavens shall be shaken."* This means it is time that our voices begin to affect the power of the heavens. It is time we begin to speak to the dwellings of the powers of God where the ordinances of God are. It is time you take the word and begin to call down the anointing from the heavens and bring down the shield of protection over your life and your home.

From where do you call forth the powers? You prophesy from the heavens because the heavens carry the dealings of the powers which are the ordinances that affect and control the smallest thing on earth.

You must arise to break the former patterns. Say, "God, I want the former patterns broken. I want the patterns of the authority of the heavens to begin to speak in my life."

The cloud is part of the heavens. When you are in the air or one a flight, prophesy to the heavens there. Tell God to knock your enemies on the ground. At least, at that point, you are in a vantage position. God decided to put the rainbow in the clouds from where the earth is controlled so that by the ordinances of that rainbow, Noah should be protected to keep his portion on earth.

Do you know that lamentations establish ordinances in heaven against the earth? When you read the book of Lamentations, you will understand the secret way of turning the powers of heaven to begin to do things on earth like in the generation of Jeremiah. It was a way of manipulation.

David took a cry and lamentations for Jonathan. He wept before the altar and cursed the people that killed Jonathan and their families. This pattern worked for David. When you read the scripture you will see how things changed for him because he sat and kept on crying and refused to be comforted even when people pleaded with him to arise. Even though people thought it was a joke, if you check the history, you will discover how that family was cursed forever.

Lamentation establishes ordinances. When Cain killed Abel, God by His law, cursed Cain. Therefore, Cain cried and lamented how he would be a fugitive everywhere he went and how men would smite him. What did God say? God put a mark on Cain so that no one would slay him.

"Then the Lord said to him, 'Not so! If anyone kills Cain, vengeance shall be taken on him sevenfold.' And the Lord put a mark on Cain, lest any who found him should attack him" (Genesis 4:13).

The mark of the Lord stops the power of negative ordinances from affecting you. It stops all those belching spirits that go around the streets speaking evil into your business and private life. It is the mark of the Lord that breaks their yoke from you. For Cain, a mark was put/ For Noah, a rainbow was set in heaven. God is going to put your remembrance in the heavens. When He remembers the covenant of righteousness which you have with Him, He will smite your enemies.

If you have suffered because of a spell, God can put a mark on you to break that spell now and repair whatever damage it may have done to your life.

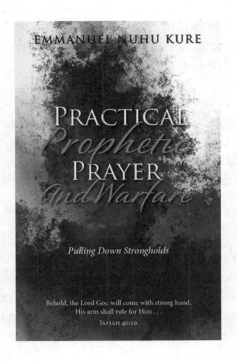

Behold, the Lord God will come with strong hand,
His arm shall rule for Him . . .
Isaiah 40:10

CHAPTER
9

PROPHESY
AND PROPHESYING

"Blow a trumpet in Zion; sound an alarm on my holy mountain! Let all the inhabitants of the land tremble, for the day of the LORD is coming; it is near, a day of darkness and gloom, a day of clouds and thick darkness! Like blackness there is spread upon the mountains a great and powerful people; their like has never been before, nor will be again after them through the years of all generations. Fire devours before them,

Chapter Nine   153

*and behind them a flame burns. The land is like the garden of
Eden before them, but behind them a desolate wilderness, and
nothing escapes them"* (Joel 2:1-3).

Let them that sleep in Zion come alive. It is time for us to
anoint ourselves with oil and rise up to prophesy according
to the ordination of the oil of God upon our heads. If you fear
the Lord and believe that God is a Spirit, allow Him to possess your entire life. God want to fill you with His fresh oil
and use you.

I wonder how many people know that our generation will not
be the last generation. After the rapture, some generations will
still be left on earth. A generation is just 50 years. Therefore,
there will still be generations after we have left in the rapture.
The Bible says there shall be no generation like the one that is
coming now meaning our own generation,

The land is like the Garden of Eden. The Garden of Eden
was soft in the hands of Adam and Eve. It neither resisted nor
harmed them. It did not make life difficult for them. Therefore, it will not make life difficult for you. Everything that is
too strong for you is about to be softened. If anything gets too
hard for you, just call for the softening by the blood of Jesus.

In verses 3 and 7 of Joel 2, the word of the Lord says:
*"A fire devoureth before them; and behind them a flame bur-
neth: they shall climb the wall like men of war; and they shall
march every one on his ways, and they shall not break their
ranks."*

It means women will raise a shout and heaven will answer.
Men will raise a cry and heaven will vomit fire. None shall
break his ranks. Everyone shall walk in his path. That means
this generation will not need to become envious and fight one

another.

We will not thrust at one another with the sword. Everyone shall be contented with his Ways. There will be no competition among ministers. We will have a common enemy - the devil himself. We are coming to the day of the unity of the Spirit and the day of the unity of faith.

Verse 9 says, *"They shall run to and fro in the city."* This last days' army raised by God is going to have a way of p e r m e - ating the whole city with their presence, filling it with their words. The Bible says, in Ezekiel 10, that the man with the linen was commanded to take the fire from within the chariot and spread it in the city.

In the Psalms, the Bible says that for our enemies to be able to control the city, they have to go to and fro every evening around the whole city releasing their belching spirits on the city and trapping your life by it.

"Then said he unto me, Son of man, these are the men that devise mischief, and give wicked counsel in this city: Which say, It is not near; let us build houses: this city is the caldron, and we be the flesh" (Ezekiel 11:2-3).

I am talking about prophesying. You have read in the Bible many times when a leader was told to "Prophesy." Whatever great thing happened up to this time in our nation's life is because some men and women have decided not to be selfish. They have decided to make themselves altars to rule the nations - not just altars that seek their own personal material blessings.

Many of us fanatically know the Lord because of the things we receive from Him - not because we want to be vessels to be used of Him. We want our self-sacrifices, our own coverings. Search yourself. Most of the prayers we pray are often more selfish than selfless.

The core of the Throne-Room Ministries is prophetic: warfare, and prophetic victories including prophetic praise. The life and the mantle of the Church in these last days is prophesy.

In Revelation, the Bible says that the testimony of our Lord Jesus Christ is the spirit of prophesy:

"And I fell at his feet to worship him. And he said unto me, See thou do it not: I am thy fellow servant, and of thy brethren that have the testimony of Jesus: worship God: for the testimony of Jesus is the spirit of prophecy" (Revelation 19:10).

Every word that comes out of your mouth, if it is the word of God, is prophesy. Your life is therefore, founded in prophesy. It is by prophesy that every ordinance of God, the harvest and missions, will be fulfilled. It is also by prophesy that our oils will be fulfilled and not run dry. Our destiny and the future of the Church lie in the spirit of prophesy as well as our ability to prophesy accurately. Spiritual accuracy is very strategic in the prophetic ministry. We must be alert and sensitive in the spirit not to allow it to degenerate to mere religious ritual.

If you want to possess a priest as well as a king, that is the order of possession. You must carry the fire of your priesthood and spread it in your city. If you are not ready to go around the city from time to time just to pray, things may be difficult for you. Notice that Isaac went into the bush just to stroll around, meditate and pray. Each time people did that in the Bible days, they stumbled into their destiny.

When you pray around the city, you are opening the gates of

the city unto yourself. But the trouble is that most of us are too lazy to do this. We are deeply involved in our businesses from 7 am to 7 pm, and we have little or no time to practice prayer. Search the Scripture from Genesis to Revelation: any man who did not have time for God never really had a destiny.

No matter who you are, if you do not make time for God, you do not have a destiny. I am talking about the time you deliberatly make for God to fulfill His call upon your life. That is, the time God uses you as His priest in the city. Many people make enough sacrifices for God to use them but without creating enough time for God to use them to fulfill His heart's desire to spread His fire in the cities.

Every watchman must make a personal discipline and commitment to "roam the streets in spiritual fellowship" like Isaiah. This is the time God pours you out as that spiritual salt on the earth. Make yourself available as a utensil for the release of the ordinances of God upon the earth. It is an order that makes you true to God and to your call. This is how the Lord holds the countries, cities and governments to ransom.

When you do this, rather than your environment holding you to ransom, you will hold it to ransom. As you do this, very often your business location will never close up to your business. The business tide will always favor your business. Your house will always have an open door because you control the atmosphere in that place. You have become the vessel that pours the oil all over the city. You have taken the fire and spread it in the City.

My beloved, can we permeate our environment (villages, towns and cities) with the fire of the Lord? It is very important that we understand these things because God is raising an army that will go to and fro in the city, not an army that will get so choked up with only its church activities to the detriment of fulfilling its Christian mandate.

There is a call on the Church that is beyond denominational and pastoral boundaries. That call is to take the cities for God. When you cannot control the spiritual atmosphere and tempo in your city, then you cannot take it. When you cannot control the lives of men in your city, you have not taken it.

Why am I saying this? You will notice that, in the Old Testament, whenever the ark of the tabernacle was taken to any battle, the battle was won. Right now, the tabernacle of the Lord is amongst men. It is in my life - it is in your life. We constitute the present-day tabernacle of God.

The Bible says in 1 Corinthians 6:19, *"...Know ye not that your body is the temple of the Holy Spirit which is in you, which ye have of God and ye are not your own?"* This means that the altar is carried in our human bodies. It means wherever the altar goes, the battle is won.

That is why the Bible says wherever the sole of your feet touches will be open to you. That was why, as they ran to and fro in the city, the city remained bound under the Lord. We must shake off laziness and run through the city.

Faith is simply stepping out to do things as ordained by God regardless of your fears and doubts. Before you rest from that obedience, the action would have fulfilled itself and blessing will follow thereafter.

God ordained Moses to become a god of the land of Egypt and the heathen. Hence He said:

"And the Lord said unto Moses, See, I have made thee a god to

Pharaoh: and Aaron thy brother shall be thy prophet" (Exodus 7:1).

Note that Pharaoh was himself a god. Therefore, for God to make a human being a god over another god meant that Moses was a type of New Testament anointing of God - the tabernacle in the hearts and lives of men, not the physical altar.

You will also notice that each time Moses went into battle, the people of Israel won. Even in his old age, when he could no longer fight, he would go there and stand in the midst of battle. As long as he stood with his hands raised up (a symbol of priesthood), Israel was victorious. By that prophetic action, he was saying, "Oh God, arise and let you enemies be scattered." Each time he got tired and brought down his hands during the battle, his people suffered defeat.

That is our problem today. We are so lazy that we do not even raise our hands. Then how can our battles be won? What do I mean? Going to and fro in the city is quite difficult for many believers to do. They do not have the time and will not create the time. Don't you know that God wants to see you in the fields, in the atmosphere speaking to things in prophetic prayer, prophetic fellowship, and prophetic cry?

Do you know that when you start praising, you are prophesying unto the Lord? Once you begin to praise and worship, you have started prophesying to the Lord. Moses knew his tabernacle had to go to the place of battle.

When the storm came against the ship where Jesus was asleep, as recorded in the Bible, when His disciples woke Him, He addressed the storm, rebuking it -- and it obeyed Him. He took His altar to the place of battle, addressed it by rebuking it, and there was a great calm..

This is an example for us to follow. After you have settled the matter in your secret place of prayer, carry the fire to the sore place that is offending your life - the place of battle. You can anoint your hands and feet and tell God that, as you make contact with the place of battle, every ordinance against your life must be terminated. You do not need to do anything that will draw attention to what you are doing as you embark on prophetic action.

If your office is in the sore place that offends your life, simply make contact with the office, the tables, the chairs, etc. By that, you are releasing the coals of fire you have picked in your secret place of prayer. You are now taking the temple with which you have fought that battle in your closet into the actual place of battle. Leave the ensign, the landmark of battle and the landmark of your victory there in the office. This has spiritual symbolism.

"And for a spirit of judgment to him that sitteth in judgment, and for strength to them that turn the battle to the gate" (Isaiah 28:6). If it is a situation that you cannot reach physically, call it and talk to it, prophesying to it. The Kingdom of God suffers violence. You must become violent in the spirit and take it by force. Find out the root of your problem, go there and set fire upon it.

You need to go to the place of battle and throw fire there. Go to and fro about the place. If you learn to do these things properly, there will not be any repercussion. The repercussion will be the normal battle that wants to stop you from your glorification.

When God has ordained victory, those battles can never win against you. That is how you soften the land. That is the meaning of the Garden of Eden being softened before Adam and

Eve. Our lives must begin to get used to carrying out prophetic prayer actions over situations.

The Joel army - the generation that will bring back King Jesus, will live and exist by prophetic prayer action. Search the Bible. Any man that never bore fruit was not called a representative of God. Anyone that bore fruit carried one prophetic action of the other.

PROPHESY AS YOU ARE COMMANDED

Note that there is a prophecy that is an instruction from God.

"So I prophesied as he commanded me, and the breath came into them, and they lived, and stood up upon their feet, an exceeding great army" (Ezekiel 37:10)..

Anytime you speak by a sudden unction, a sudden revelation, you are not in charge. God drops the revelation and you say it as you feel it. That is what is referred to as a gift of prophesy.

When a man prophesies, it does not necessarily mean that he has the gift of prophesy. In the Old Testament, Saul prophesied without having the gift of prophecy. Therefore, when you successfully prophesy once, it does not mean that you have the gift of prophesy. However, this can be developed. There is the prophecy that is a gift and there is one that is just a fellowship.

This one can call forth the one that is ordinary prophecy. When you have the gift of prophecy, you have an inclination to notice easily what other do not notice. This means that your senses can easily detect when something is wrong with the atmosphere.

It is on that foundation that the gift of prophecy is properly built. When the gift of prophecy comes, it can either allow you knowledge into the future or the present or the past. The present knowledge must be involved. From there, God takes you either to the past or future, thus using the present as a catalyst. The spirit of prophecy is built upon the fertile grounds of sensitivity to the present.

In Ezekiel 37:1-3, the spirit took Ezekiel to the valley of dry bones.

"The hand of the Lord was upon me, and carried me out in the spirit of the Lord, and set me down in the midst of the valley which was full of bones, And caused me to pass by them round about: and, behold, there were very many in the open valley; and, lo, they were very dry. And he said unto me, Son of man, can these bones live? And I answered, O Lord God, thou knowest."

The Spirit carried him to where the problem was. He did not leave him in his house. In prophetic prayer action, we go to the place and the point of concern - the place in focus.

Remember, Elisha called the young man and gave him oil to anoint Jehu.

"And Elisha the prophet called one of the children of the prophets, and said unto him, Gird up thy loins, and take this box of oil in thine hand, and go to Ramothgilead:.. look out there Jehu the son of Jehoshaphat.. Then take the box of oil, and pour it on his head, and say, Thus saith the LORD, I have anointed thee king over Israel." (2 Kings 9:1-3).

All that was needed for Jehu was a contact with oil and the word. When the word is prophesied, it makes people and situations do what God wants. It is bringing the influence of the word of God upon people and situations subjecting them to His word.

It was the same thing Elijah did by casting a mantle on Elisha. From that time, even without saying a word, Elisha starting following Elijah. That was a prophetic prayer. action.

That situation in your life that has defied solution all these years may only be waiting for a prophetic prayer action. Begin to pray in this manner and keep it up until the situation changes.

The Bible says, *"The children of this world are wiser than the children of the Kingdom,"* Prophetic praying belongs to us but we have lost it to unbelievers, apparently because of ignorance or laziness. I pray that the Lord will bring you out of every prison that has hitherto hindered you from operating in the prophetic.

If someone casts a spell on your car, which has resulted in incessant breakdowns of your car, it possibly means be has done prophetic praying against you. It is your responsibility and Kingdom right to break that scepter of wickedness over you and your property, and do a "return match."

Carry the battle to the gate. If they come to your house to do it, go to their houses to do it too, for the Lord is strength to them that carry the battle to the gate. If you cannot get to their houses, use one of their properties as a point of contact to return their spell to them and add your own burdens on their heads. This will serve as a padlock to lock them up in the spirit and check their satanic retaliation.

God took Ezekiel in the spirit and told him what to do. Verse

2 of Ezekiel 37 says, *"And caused me to pass by them round about."* He went around them - he encircled them. In prayer, if God takes you somewhere and instructs you on what to do, go ahead and do it. It shall come to pass. Does that remind you of the wall of Jericho?

The Bible says clearly in the verses below that demonic people control the city by going around it belching out of their mouth.

"They return at evening: they make a noise like a dog, and go round about the city. Behold, they belch out with their mouth: swords are in their lips: for who, say they, doth hear?" (Psalm 59:6-7)

This is spiritual warfare. If a house in your village is disturbing you, go to that village and greet everybody normally. Then encircle the house once to release the fire of God on it. Your deliverance will come speedily. In verses 3-4 of Ezekiel 37, God says, "Prophecy." The only solution to dead situations is prophecy. Therefore, prophesy to any dead situation in your life.

What do you prophesy to the dry bones? The word of God, which the Bible says is in your heart and in your mouth. Therefore, open the verses of the Scripture relevant to the situation and read them aloud to the situation. Do not prophesy in your heart. The Bible says, "Confession is made unto salvation." Speak out and say, "Hear, Oh earth, heaven, etc.," depending on the issue at hand and then pronounce the word to whatever it is.

After that, you can say with authority on the basis of the foundation of the life in this scripture, "I command you in Jesus' Name." Learn to prophesy the word of God with authority over adverse circumstances in our life.

TO WHAT DO YOU PROPHESY?

1) Prophesy to yourself:

"The Spirit of the Lord is upon me, because he hath anointed me to preach the gospel to the poor; he hath sent me to heal the brokenhearted, to preach deliverance to the captives, and recovering of sight to the blind, to set at liberty them that are bruised, To preach the acceptable year of the Lord... And he began to say unto them, This day is this scripture fulfilled in your ears" (Luke 4:18, 19, 21).

When you prophesy to yourself, you appropriate the word of God to your life. That is, you anoint yourself with the word of God. Read the word to yourself, and your life will change. In the Scripture, Jesus kept on reminding the people what God spoke concerning Him through the prophets. He was not only appropriating but also renewing His commission by the word. When you anoint yourself with the word, you renew your commission by it.

When Jesus read the prophecy concerning Him, the first thing He said to them was, "Today, this scripture is fulfilled in your ears." Immediately when He said that, anointing came upon Him for His ministry to begin that day. Every word He spoke there began to stir Him up. In this way, He activated the oil upon Him.

You can do that for your own life too. Open the Bible to where God has spoken concerning you. Read it to yourself and say, "God, your word says this concerning me today and I receive it. This day, is this Scripture fulfilled in my life."

When you do that, the gifts of God will begin to well up within you unto manifestation. You will begin to operate naturally in the prophetic. Why? Because that is the pathway the Master set for you. It was the pathway for His own ordination. When you do that, you are ordaining yourself not by the laying on of hands by men, but directly by the Spirit of God. You need that. You can prophesy to anoint yourself with the word of God.

2) Prophesy to your fellow man:
By this I mean anybody apart from yourself - from your immediate family members like your spouse, children, to your neighbors, collogues, business associates, friends, etc. It is here, you address the cauldron:

In Genesis, God says He will require your blood from man and from beasts:

"And surely your blood of your lives will I require; at the hand of every beast will I require it, and at the hand of man; at the hand of every man's brother will I require the life of man" (Genesis 9:5).

3) You can prophesy also to the earth or the land:
"Therefore, ye mountains of Israel, hear the word of the Lord God; Thus saith the Lord God to the mountains, and to the hills, to the rivers, and to the valleys, to the desolate wastes, and to the cities that are forsaken, which became a prey and derision to the residue of the heathen that are round about; Therefore thus saith the Lord God; Surely in the fire of my jealousy have I spoken against the residue of the heathen, and against all Idumea, which have appointed my land into their possession with the joy of all their heart, with despiteful minds, to cast it out for a prey" (Ezekiel 36:4-5).

We see God in the above scripture prophesying to the land. You can do the same, telling the land directly to hear the word of the Lord. You can prophesy to the earth about your own affairs, about God, your fellow men as well as spirits. You can tell the earth to disregard the spirit world when they act contrary to God's plan for your life.

4) Prophesy to the spirit world:
This includes the astral world, the metaphysical world, the world of astrology, the telepathic world, the world of the mind and everything superficial and elemental. Prophesy to thrones: the throne of God as well as the throne of Satan.

You can prophesy to spirits after their order of rulership: principalities, power, dominions, etc. There is a throne of righteousness that you can prophesy to come and protect you.

In Ephesians 3:10-11, the Bible says that the eternal purpose of God is for the Church to declare the manifold wisdom of God to the kingdom of darkness.

"To the intent that now unto the principalities and powers in heavenly places might be known by the church the manifold wisdom of God, According to the eternal purpose which he purposed in Christ Jesus our Lord."

The only way the Church can declare the manifold wisdom of God is through the spirit of prophesy and revelation.

5) Prophesy to altars:
Altars are different from thrones. A throne is a symbol of authority and rulership while an altar is where you make contact with the supernatural. It is also where you are empowered to release your decrees, your oils, the unction that works for you. It is a place of spiritual contact.

Prophesy to the altar as in 1 Kings:
"And, behold, there came a man of God out of Judah by the word of the LORD unto Bethel: and Jeroboam stood by the altar to burn incense. And he cried against the altar in the word

of the LORD, and said, O altar, altar, thus saith the LORD; Behold, a child shall be born unto the house of David, Josiah by name; and upon thee shall he offer the priests of the high places that burn incense upon thee, and men's bones shall be burnt upon thee. And he gave a sign the same day, saying, This is the sign which the LORD hath spoken; Behold, the altar shall be rent, and the ashes that are upon it shall be poured out. And it came to pass, when king Jeroboam heard the saying of the man of God, which had cried against the altar in Bethel, that he put forth his hand from the altar, saying, Lay hold on him. And his hand, which he put forth against him, dried up, so that he could not pull it in again to him. The altar also was rent, and the ashes poured out from the altar, according to the sign which the man of God had given by the word of the LORD" (1 Kings 13:1-5).

You can prophesy to the altars of idolatry, witchcraft, divination, occultism, etc., in your environment, and they will obey and bow.

6) Prophesy to the winds:
In Ezekiel 37, God commanded the prophet Ezekiel to prophesy to the winds.

"Then said he unto me, Prophesy unto the wind, prophesy, son of man, and say to the wind, Thus saith the Lord God; Come from the four winds, O breath, and breathe upon these slain, that they may live. So I prophesied as he commanded me, and the breath came into them, and they lived, and stood up upon their feet, an exceeding great army" (Ezekiel 37:9-10).

You can prophesy to the winds to reverse the curse in your life and bring you a blessing instead.

7) Prophesy also to the Lord:
You do this in praise and worship.

8) Prophesy to the elements, the creation:

Prophesy to the elements of creation to control your environment. By earthly elements, we are referring to water, fire and air. But in the Bible, by elements of creation we are referring to the winds (air), water, dust and the blood.

When the Lord said He would curse the land of Israel, He said He would make the land mix with the blood so that the land could be cursed. Why mix it with the blood? This is because the land exists by the blood. The Bible says there is life in the blood. Therefore, you can prophesy to the elements of creation as revealed by the Bible.

Blood takes in oxygen. Have you ever thought that the oxygen in the blood contains the elements of the Spirit of God present at creation? Have you ever thought that part of the elements that keep your blood alive is the Spirit in your breath which flows around the blood too?

Many people think that their spirit dwells only in their soul but do not know that their spirit also dwells in their blood. There is a relationship between your blood and your spirit. Are you aware that your soul is in your blood?

Everyone is empty without Jesus Christ because He is the Spirit of life. When you have the Spirit of life in you, you have Him in your blood.

9) Prophesy to the nations

"O Zion, that bringest good tidings, get thee up into the high mountain; O Jerusalem, that bringest good tidings, lift up thy voice with strength; lift it up, be not afraid; say unto the cities of Judah, Behold your God!" "Also, thou son of man, prophesy unto the mountains of Israel, and say, Ye mountains of Israel, hear the word of the LORD." "Set ye up a standard

in the land, blow the trumpet among the nations, prepare the nations against her, call together against her the kingdoms of Ararat, Minni, and Ashchenaz; appoint a captain against her; cause the horses to come up as the rough caterpillers" (Isaiah 40:9; Ezekiel 36:1; Jeremiah 51:27).

Sometimes you need to sit over your nation in prayer and begin to call that which is in the earth to be replaced by that which is from the heavens. As you prophesy and call forth, open the gates of your nation and the gates of heaven, events will begin to change. This is the mystery of divine replacement. You must carry the prophetic exercise as a cry and make it become the obligation of heaven.

"So I prophesied as I was commanded: and as I prophesied, there was a noise, and behold a shaking, and the bones came together, bone to his bone. And when I beheld, lo, the sinews and the flesh came up upon them, and the skin covered them above: but there was no breath in them. Then said he unto me, Prophesy unto the wind, prophesy, son of man, and say to the wind, Thus saith the Lord GOD; Come from the four winds, O breath, and breathe upon these slain, that they may live. So I prophesied as he commanded me, and the breath came into them, and they lived, and stood up upon their feet, an exceeding great army" (Ezekiel 37:7-10).

You can prophesy to forest fields (Ezekiel 20:46), to waters, to the winds, to the land (Ezekiel 36:6), to the mountains, caves and rocks, etc. You can virtually prophesy to everything that God has created. You have the authority to prophesy blessings to bless and to bring redemption to creations like Ezekiel did. In the same vein, you have authority to prophesy curses to curse and to being judgment over every evil work of the enemy.

Follow the patterns in Ezekiel 36:

"Son of man, set thy face toward the south, and drop thy word toward the south, and prophesy against the forest of the south field." "Prophesy therefore concerning the land of Israel, and say unto the mountains, and to the hills, to the rivers, and to the valleys, Thus saith the Lord God; Behold, I have spoken in my jealousy and in my fury, because ye have borne the shame of the heathen: Therefore thus saith the Lord God; I have lifted up mine hand, Surely the heathen that are about you, they shall bear their shame" (Ezekiel 20:46; 36:6-7).

Annually, or once in a while, nations, peoples and ethnic groups need to gather before the God of heaven and repent, confess and make fresh covenants between their people and the God of heaven. They should do this for their sons and daughters, for their harvests and for their prosperity, for peace in the kingdom, for their kings and generations, following the patterns of the book of Nehemiah and Ezra. The nations or tribes that do this shall find great favor before God.

Care must be taken to make Jesus the central focus without which it should not be done at all. Families can come together to confess their sins of idolatry; to break the covenants of their fathers with demons. They must dissociate themselves from those covenants in prayer and declare the Lordship of Jesus Christ alone over their families in a new covenant with the Lord.

This will affect the glory and visitations of such families. As they meet in family meetings, they can re-examine their lives in the light of the word of God, and admonish the younger ones to abstain from evil and follow after things that are pleasing to the Lord. I am confidently sure that wherever this is sincerely done, a memorial will be written for that family in heaven as it was in the case of Abraham.

Nations, tribes and families can receive great blessings if they learn the secret of covenant making with the God of heaven through our Lord Jesus Christ. Let the fire of heaven fall on you as you read this book. And let His Kingdom come in you afresh. Amen.

10) Blowing trumpets over cities:

"And the LORD shall be seen over them, and his arrow shall go forth as the lightning: and the Lord God shall blow the trumpet, and shall go with whirlwinds of the south. The LORD of hosts shall defend them; and they shall devour, and subdue with sling stones; and they shall drink, and make a noise as through wine; and they shall be filled like bowls, and as the corners of the altar. And the LORD their God shall save them in that day as the flock of his people: for they shall be as the stones of a crown, lifted up as an ensign upon his land" (Zechariah 9:14-16).

As a watchman unto the Lord over your city, you could take your trumpet and blow it over the city from its walls or gates or borders. Then, you are opening the heavens and the mysteries of it upon that cry. You will be calling forth the Mighty Judge and the Prince of Peace to come forth and act speedily, releasing the winds of healing and the breath of God by the way of the Holy Spirit.

He releases you to sound the trumpet. Trumpets are used to call forth, to gather and to release. Blowing the trumpet is a declaration that something is happening. It is a call to the gates of heaven for the dwellings of God to be opened. The prophetic march over Jericho was never complete without the trumpets.

Sometimes, get trumpets with loudspeakers and blow them around the city, on every major road. And let a loud voice sound over the speaker saying, "Repent, for the Kingdom of God is at hand. Repent! Jesus is coming soon. Accept Him!" Behold, Jesus sitting on the conscience of the people by your proclamations and let the Holy Spirit do the harvesting.

When you do these things, the altars of darkness and their grip over the city will dissolve. It is time for us to pay the price for the revival and the expected harvest, and ultimately for the second coming of Jesus Christ. It might cost some lives. But it will give many lives eternal salvation and establish Jesus as Lord over the land. It will also hasten His coming.

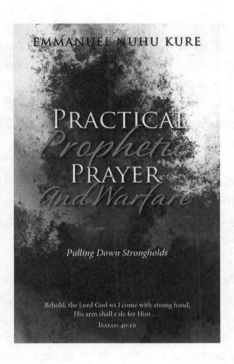

CHAPTER 10

STRANGE VISIONS AND PROPHECIES

GOD **DOES NOT** commune with any child of His except upon an altar. That is why in the Old Testament, any time they wanted to call upon the Lord, they built an altar from where they called Him. The children of Israel had to first build an altar because the Bible says, "Upon that altar of merry would I commune with you.

Chapter Ten   175

"And thou shalt put the mercy seat above upon the ark; and in the ark thou shalt put the testimony that I shall give thee. And there I will meet with thee, and I will commune with thee from above the mercy seat, from between the two cherubims which are upon the ark of the testimony, of all things which I will give thee in commandment unto the children of Israel" (Exodus 25:21-22).

The secret of covenant offering is laying your life before the Lord. With this, you have established an altar by which He can keep you alive. Bear in mind that God never reaches to us and never communes with us except upon an altar.

It is after you have put the testimony inside the ark that the Lord shall meet with you and commune with you. Inside our own altar, we need to put the testimony that He would give us. It means transferring that word of God into the altar, that is your flesh and into your spirit. It means studying, memorizing and attempting to remember the word of God at every instance. You should strive to feed your heart with His word.

No matter how much of God's word I read, the day He does not give me a revelation. I don't get any revelation from His word. This has been my experience with Him. It is not by the volume of the word I study or the level of prayer I pray or even by coming apart in fasting that I get revelation. But it is by consistent storing His word in my heart that God draws my attention to what He is about to do or say. So I make a conscious effort to feed my spirit with the word of God every day. Sometimes it could be difficult. But you have to beat your flesh and put it under for your spirit man to remain above.

COUNTERFEIT VISIONS AND DREAMS

Every counterfeit dream will contradict the word of God. If you have such dreams, throw them out. It is an antichrist spirit or a product of your mind at work to deceive you. Do not receive it. It will ruin your life. Do not force it on your Church whoever you are. Judge every vision or dream. X-ray it thoroughly until it stands the test of the Scriptures. It may be a familiar spirit at work or a mere abundance of the inspiration of your spirit. Certainly not the Spirit of God.

Note that there is a big difference between your spirit and His Spirit. Your spirit can be right when the word guides it. The inspiration you get can be perfectly correct when the word guides it. Often, the Lord speaks to you through your spirit and not necessarily through the word. He uses your spirit and gives you an unction that takes you away from trouble. He makes your spirit to reject an environment or an individual.

When He impresses that on you and you do not work contrary you will be saved. However, when you insist on your own way, He will smite you because you have broken the hedge. This is because the testimony of the Lord has a way of guiding the human spirit. Yet the human spirit and its unction never takes the place of the voice of the Holy Spirit.

Today, the Church has replaced the voice of God with the human unction. Most people who think they are practicing prophecy are actually replacing the voice of God with their human voice.

It is not every revelation that God gives me that comes to pass immediately. There are some minor ones that do come to pass unnoticed. However, when it comes to major revelation that may probably cause me trouble or ruin my integrity, I am careful enough to make sure I hear clearly. I must be sure that it is not the voice of my spirit.

I believe in the sacred secret oils. But I do not believe in glorying in the oils because they are not mine. I am just a carrier. The day I disappoint God, He will take it away and I will fall. Since I know that I am not indispensable, I do not glory in it. The Master exclusively owns it.

It is from the stored word that the Lord tells you sacred things. He uses His stored word as a stepping stone to letting you know those things. When you hear me speak those prophesies, I must have heard from another voice (God's voice) apart from my own, and I must have heard clearly.

Most of the utterances I make are not by faith but by sight. I hear, I see, I speak. It is not the figment of my imagination. So I can stand by them anywhere because the Lord has spoken. There are times when I speak and get frightened of what I hear, see and speak because the Bible warns about false prophets who speak from their imagination - from the guidance of their own hearts just to please people.

"Then the Lord said unto me, The prophets prophesy lies in my name: I sent them not, neither have I commanded them, neither spake unto them: they prophesy unto you a false vision and divination, and a thing of nought, and the deceit of their heart. Therefore thus saith the Lord concerning the prophets that prophesy in my name, and I sent them not, yet they say, Sword and famine shall not be in this land; By sword and famine shall those prophets be consumed" (Jeremiah 14:14-15).

The Lord said He would punish false prophets with bitter food and give them poison to drink. It is because of them that wickedness fills the land. He will not spare their families either.

PROPHESY WITH BOLDNESS
Prophecy should be spoken with boldness, though with due respect.

"But prophesy not again any more at Bethel: for it is the king's chapel, and it is the king's court. Then answered Amos, and said to Amaziah, I was no prophet, neither was I a prophet's son; but I was an herdman, and a gatherer of sycomore fruit: And the Lord took me as I followed the flock, and the Lord said unto me, Go, prophesy unto my people Israel" (Amos 7:13-15).

Here, the prophet did not mince words in telling the king his message.

The Lord once sent me to Abuja to pass some words to the authorities there. I went, bowed (Paul said, "I became all things to all men that I might draw some to Christ") and delivered the message as I was instructed from above. Whoever the Lord gives me a message for, I will deliver the message intact with urgency and accuracy as given, regardless of the consequences. No message from God should be delivered by proxy under whatever condition unless the Lord specifically said to.

Some of us have deflated our unction by the reason of our mouth. As a result, we make no impact when we speak because we have already messed up ourselves.

You do not have to tell friends or close relatives when you get a specific message from the Lord for somebody because they might discourage you from executing what the Lord instructed you to do since the message is not for them. If you do, you will be violating spiritual laws. However, you may let them know after the assignment is done.

It is time to bring up mature Christians who will be able to prophesy boldly, no matter how unpleasant the prophesy may be to the recipients. We have so many immature Christians in the Church today. They slow down the advancement of the Church and the Kingdom of God. Over-zealous people are everywhere, many of them can be classified along Nadab and Abihu who took incense to burn before Moses saying, "Thus says the Lord, 'We too can prophesy'" As they burnt the incense, they became like Gehazi. They are actually making spiritual input. But unfortunately, it will never move the Kingdom forward because there is no spiritual order in what they are doing.

Instead of moving the Church forward, they would continue to stand in God's way. But God is a God of order and would only give His approval when things are done decently and in order. The Church must come out of this trap. Some Christians need to die further, just like the apostle Paul, so that they can know the glory of the Lord.

If you want to kill me fast, touch the ministry. If you fight against me as an individual, I will survive. But when you try to stifle the word or stop the anointing or block it by all means, I will begin to withdraw and ask God to defend His anointing. When God is too slow for me, I will die fast. Elisha died of a broken heart because he felt the Lord in one thing, had not answered his prayer.

Let me say this again: it is on the altar that God communes. In Zechariah's case, it was while he was yet serving before the Lord on the altar that the Lord appeared to release John. Similarly, it was while Isaiah stood in the Lord's temple doing God's service that he saw the Lord high and lifted up. He was ushered into the "committee meeting" where God decided that a Savior must be sent to earth.

If you make your altar complete - putting your testimony and divorcing your spirit from interfering with God's Spirit - He will begin to drop revelations into your spirit. I have discovered that until men know how to distinguish between revelations, they will continue to get into trouble.

Some ministers of the gospel mix up revelations today because they have not learned to distinguish between revelations from their spirit and revelations that emanate from the Spirit of God. Everything they get inspired about they say, "Thus says the Lord," or "The Lord spoke to me," when God may not have said anything.

It is a misnomer to think that the Lord speaks every time. Some would merely speak in tongues and say, "Thus says the Lord..." God does not operate in this way. Our visions have led us to lose track many times. This is why some ministers believe they are serving God when they are not. Their "visions" have led them astray. Yet they would not listen to God's counsel.

Some people get married on the wrong premise, driven by their lust. Yet they say it is the Holy Spirit because they had feelings. Churches are being broken apart by prophecies. For example, it is common to find somebody who comes up and says, "I saw in the spirit that the pastor's wife is a demon." So, what does the pastor do? Kill the wife or send her packing? Of course not. This should not happen in the Church. Every revelation must pass through the divine scrutiny of the infallible word of God.

Abigail married Nabal who was a fool. Who killed Nabal? God. And God chose when to take away Nabal. Let God judge. For pastors who think they have married the wrong wives, their wives' faithfulness will decide their destiny. Do not fear those things. They are decided in heaven. Also, note that her own faithfulness will save her. That is the balanced word.

The Church must not allow visions to kill her. It is the ploy of the devil to destroy us. Hence, he comes with the counterfeit of the divine realities that guarantee the advancement of the Kingdom of God. Homes and ministries are being divided by false visions and dreams.

Ministers of God, beware of strange visions! Congregations, stop passing strange visions and dreams in the name of spirituality. Even if you fasted for 100 days, it is not every dream that is from the Lord. Some of them come because of "tomato anointing" - you got so hungry that you started seeing stars.

BEWARE OF STRANGE VISIONS

I believe in visions. But the point I am making is, Beware of strange visions! Like Paul said, "If anybody prophesies, I prophesy more." Nevertheless, I am conscious that if you are not careful, your prophecy can bring you down. Do not obey visions and prophecies foolishly. They can bring you down. God is patient with you to come around and see it clearly. God does not begin to punish you immediately if you have not acted immediately.

If God wanted you to pack out of a particular place within 24 hours, for example, He would have started giving you the indication before the person who brought you the prophecy confirms it. I do not obey till I hear clearly, especially when it has to do with one's destiny.

I have been given keys to houses in Port Harcourt and told, "Thus says the Lord, come and stay with us." If I had obeyed without hearing clearly, I would have been ruined a long time ago. There are some gifts you should reject if the Spirit of God is not in them. When you win a major battle against hell, you get promoted afterwards.

Please beware of visions. They can make or kill you. Be careful to distinguish a vision coming from your spirit or from unction or from dreams or what the Lord said. Dreams are not always perfect. In fact, they are not perfect. Dreams often only warn you about the real thing without telling you what that real thing is.

Visions tell you the real thing, like "This man has fornicated. He did last week in this place." When you cross-check, you will discover that it is true. That is vision.

In dreams, you need interpretation because what you saw was a shadow of the real thing. With dreams, you have to be more careful than with visions. Otherwise, you will oftentimes make mistakes in interpretation which can destroy your relationship with many people because you have unguardedly rushed to unravel the dream.

Visions are specific. But in some cases, they are incorrect. Learn to differentiate between visions and dreams in your life. Do not operate dreams as laws. Pray about them and test them. Please, be aware that visions and dreams can ultimately destroy the glory of the Church and your anointing. Sone men who would have become great prophets were destroyed by the immature way they handled their dreams at a younger age. Hence they could not become prophets.

The young prophet in 1 Kings 13 was not wise in handling a contrary vision from the old prophet. He consequently perished.

"And when he was gone, a lion met him by the way, and slew him: and his carcase was cast in the way, and the ass stood by it, the lion also stood by the carcase... And when the prophet that brought him back from the way heard thereof, he said,

It is the man of God, who was disobedient unto the word of the Lord: therefore the Lord hath delivered him unto the lion, which hath torn him, and slain him, according to the word of the Lord, which he spake unto him" (1 Kings 13:24, 26).

Notice that not all the sons of the prophets became prophets. Very few were able to breakthrough. The reason was that they kept mixing up revelations. That is why they never saw the light of day. The same reason accounts for why we have many prophets today but few breakthroughs to the place of glory.

We all need to grow. The Bible says now we know a little. But when we behold His face, we grow from glory to glory, from grace to grace. Therefore, do not allow the little you know now to become a snare and suddenly destroy you. Continue to grow. I am still growing. There are things I am learning. Beware, knowledge puffs up.

I have stood up in some meetings to speak but where God refused to talk. It was not my fault. If I stand to talk and God refuses to talk, He must have His good reasons. I am not God and I cannot force a message when there is none.

It is not because I have not studied the Bible. I always study it. But the revelation may just not come. God must come upon the testimony and commune with you. Do not just take a testimony and begin to speak it. It is what you speak out that becomes a revelation.

"Then said Jesus unto them, When ye have lifted up the Son of man, then shall ye know that I am he, and that I do nothing of myself; but as my Father hath taught me, I speak these things. And he that sent me is with me: the Father hath not left me alone; for I do always those things that please him" (John 8:28-29).

How do you know the Father is with you? You know through what happens whenever you lift Him up. What does it mean to lift up the Son of man? It means exalting Him at all times, no matter the situation. He must have preeminence in all things.

For instance, when God suddenly shows up in a seemingly hopeless situation to turn the tide in your favor, it means He has all along been with you. This causes His Name to be lifted up. If a man is not delivered in the day of trouble, possibly God is not with him at that material time. But if he is saved from trouble, it is a possible sign that the Father is with him.

Your anointing and acceptability to God is rested and proved in the day of trouble. If He allows you to rot in it, then something might be wrong somewhere in your fellowship with Him. Talking about getting into trouble, I do not mean self-inflicted troubles or troubles we find ourselves in as a result of our foolishness and presumptuousness. I mean troubles inflicted by the enemy. Elisha's trouble was self-inflicted. So, if you are in trouble today, as a child of God, be assured that the Father will take you out of it.

There are people who were once on the right track but who have today been derailed by false visions. You need to go back and check where you left the reality of the Lord's calling. Vision is one of the easiest ways by which a man sometimes leaves the pathway of God's calling. A man's life is confused by multitudes of visions.

You must differentiate between the genuine and the counterfeit, and be courageous enough to separate both.

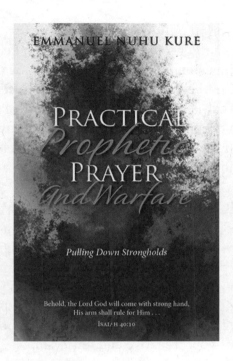

CHAPTER
11

PROPHETIC OFFERINGS
Normal Offerings

OFFERINGS SPEAK. **WHEN** you give, you are sending a voice, an advocacy for your situation. If you give in
righteousness, with the right mind attitude and motive, you
have succeeded in building an altar and a voice for yourself in
heaven by your offering.

An offering scripturally represents or stands for the owner. Therefore, when you give, what you give reflects your life, its worth and its situation. Cain as a person, was not acceptable before God because his representative offering was not acceptable. That is, he did not give the best of his worth to God. A lot of people are not accepted because, as a habit, they do not give the best of their worth to God. This is the average kind of offering the Church gives to God now.

OFFERING OF LOVE AND FELLOWSHIP

Secondly, people give not as a fellowship and a sign of worship and love for the Master, but because of situations and what they expect to get in return. When you give bountiful and sumptuous offerings unto the Lord out of your love for the Master without any pressure on you, it stands for you as a vow unto the Lord in the day of trouble. The Lord remembers it as a proof of your true love and fellowship.

The woman in Luke 7:37 did not expect to be noticed or acknowledged. She adored her God with all that she was worth. Her sacrificial offering spoke and drew Jesus' attention to her. It was her soul speaking.

"And, behold, a woman in the city, which was a sinner, when she knew that Jesus sat at meat in the Pharisee's house, brought an alabaster box of ointment, And stood at his feet behind him weeping, and began to wash his feet with tears, and did wipe them with the hairs of her head, and kissed his feet, and anointed them with the ointment... And he turned to the woman, and said unto Simon, Seest thou this woman? I entered into thine house, thou gavest me no water for my feet: but she hath washed my feet with tears, and wiped them with the hairs of her head. Thou gavest me no kiss: but this woman since the time I came in hath not ceased to kiss my feet. My head with oil thou didst not anoint: but this woman hath

anointed my feet with ointment. Wherefore I say unto thee, Her sins, which are many, are forgiven; for she loved much: but to whom little is forgiven, the same loveth little. And he said unto her, Thy sins are forgiven" (Luke 7:37-38, 44-48).

Jesus adopted the woman for her sacrificial offering. That is one of the things you gain by this kind of offering. It brings about adoption. The Lord takes over you as His. This is one aspect of the prophetic offerings that brings about **ADOPTION**. It establishes a fellowship between Father and Son. From that point, that woman became Jesus' responsibility. This kind of offering, whether big or small, makes you Jesus' responsibility. I desire to see this kind of offering becoming our normal way of life in our relationship with God.

DESPERATE COVENANT OFFERING

The other kind of prophetic offering is the one that stops the gates of hell prevailing against you. I call it the Desperate Covenant Offering. It sets off a red alert in heaven on your behalf.

It is a desperate cry for immediate intervention to save a person from an immediate danger when he is suddenly trapped between life-threatening evils that may or may not necessarily be his making. This kind of offering must be preceded with a desperate cry for mercy, broken confessions and restitution if God must answer.

The event in 1 Chronicles 2:1 was a quick, desperate offering from David at the threshing floor of Oman to stop the angel of destruction from completely annihilating Jerusalem. Note that it was the angel of the Lord who, moved by David's repentance, told Gad (David's seer) how to escape the spirit of destruction. This is a Holy Spirit teaching for escaping desperate situations.

Zipporah stopped the sword from descending on Moses when she immediately sacrificed the foreskin of her son. Abigail saved Nabal's life by the offering she gave David. There is a pattern of salvation in the Bible when fat desperate offerings are made unto the Lord. The size of the problem dictates the size of the offering. It must be an offering that pains you, commensurate with the pains you are going through. That is, it must cost you something. David said that, "God frobid that I give God what cost me nothing."

"All this, O king, doth Araunah give unto the king. And Araunah said unto the king, Jehovah thy God accept thee. And the king said unto Araunah, Nay; but I will verily buy it of thee at a price. Neither will I offer burnt-offerings unto Jehovah my God which cost me nothing. So David bought the threshing-floor and the oxen for fifty shekels of silver" (2 Samuel 24:23-24 ASV).

Many of us give from convenience rather than from a real sacrifice that digs very deep into our resources. If it costs you nothing, you should not expect God to bother about what does not bother you. We must strip ourselves of the "self" if we want results in our relationship with God. If the Church must become invincible, we must begin to do the right things the right way.

You need to understand that every offering speaks. Therefore, you must always prophesy (pray) over your offerings before you give them. Whether it is a kobo or a million Naira, a cent or a million dollars, pray over it knowing that it is an expression of your love and situation, a sharing of your life with the Master.

It is an intercourse with the Master where you give Him the best side of you. Don't ever think of the value of any amount of money you give out of the liberty of your spirit. We have the mandate of the Scriptures to give cheerfully rather than under pressure or necessity. Pray your love, adoration and thanksgiving over it before giving it. This will always work wonders for you in the heart of God.

COVENANT WEALTH

Some people have been called to be custodians of God's treasures (wealth) for the fulfillment of His programs on earth. Actually, in the prophetic program of God for the Church, as well as the Scripture, when God declares a man physically or financially rich, such a man turns out to be, indeed, the richest man in his society.

The men we call rich, money-wise, are not actually seen to be so in heaven. A man who wants to control the kind of riches God speaks of, that is to become richer than whole nations like Job, Abraham, Isaac, Jacob, David or Solomon. That person must learn to fit into and fulfil God's program for His Church and the coming of Jesus Christ.

He should not act simply as a big man deciding who or who not to do charity for. His attitude should not be that of "helping" the Church. No. God does not want help. God wants you to be an extension of His program. You are like a conduit pipe for the supply of His oil to His Church. You are His workmanship created in Christ Jesus to fulfil His program.

If you develop this attitude, you will only give where He commands you whether in your major tithes, ordinary or desperate offerings, thanksgiving offerings, peace offerings or love (worship) offerings. Every amount you give should be channeled into fulfilling the program or plan of a major project of God. It must be channeled into making the Church effective and irreproachable.

We grieve God the way we give these days. We are not supposed to scatter our money indiscriminately in the name of giving to God. The Bible tells us that:

"Take heed to thyself that thou offer not thy burnt-offerings in every place that thou seest; but in the place which Jehovah shall choose in one of thy tribes, there thou shalt offer thy burnt-offerings, and there thou shalt do all that I command thee" (Deuteronomy 12:13-14).

The Lord chooses the specific place for the fulfilment of a particular part of His program. Stop distributing one offering into so many places in bits and pieces. Besides being unscriptural, it robs you of a memorial in heaven. In the bid to make themselves relevant, in every place and with every man they meet, many people rob themselves of their place and glory with God.

When they have an offering, they make sure that every major minister they relate with, as well as their ministries, get a little share. They use this to solicit prayers, and sometimes recognition, from the ministries or ministers. But this only nullifies the efficacy of the word of God to being blessings and to fulfil God's program. That is why such people return to their past problems and struggles.

When you give a large offering to a particular project, mission field, church program, for administrative purposes, or a building project (which God has commanded you to give into) - that gift will raise a major memorial for God on earth.

God may have been groaning that a particular project be accomplished, raising people and committing money into it. However, the person giving the money can derail his memorial if he either becomes reluctant to give due to a flamboyant lifestyle or he may give to impress men and win their recognition.

Let me make it clear as God's prophetic voice in this generation, that once a need is registered in a place in heaven, God sets out to raise people on earth to fulfill that need. He opens doors for them only because of that particular need. And when they dissipate their money recklessly, God's will for setting out to bless them is hindered because His project is not fulfilled.

Consequently, God looks for substitutes. He keeps searching until He finds men who understand this principle of heaven. That is why there are not very many rich men in the Church. It is not because their righteousness makes it difficult for them to be rich in a corrupt society. It is because they do not meet God's standards in the days they were tested by heaven.

You must understand and get this heavenly principle right. God only gives in response to a need (His need) in His Church. He picks people that will fulfil that need, and opens the gates of heaven unto them as channels to advance His work.

But they grieve Him when, instead of fulfilling that project, they satisfy their own desire and buy for themselves recognition. It is imperative for the Church to realize that God specifically sends money to fulfil or complete particular projects.

Accordingly, we need to submit as channels or fronts for God to fulfil those particular projects even in the midst of distractions and temptations to divert the funds and seek recognition for oneself. It is then that the Church can begin to raise great men of great wealth who will fulfil the work before Jesus comes.

Where are the disciplined men who will keep covenant with God and establish God's patterns and Kingdom on earth? Could it be that your money or goods got stuck in some places because you have not fulfilled the particular purpose for which you were blessed?

Whatever money is sent from heaven has a specific purpose for which it was sent. Does your money fulfil that specific purpose? Or is it sparingly spread to fulfill too many purposes? There is the need for confession, repentance and restitution so that God can start with you afresh and reorganize your life. When this is done, we will begin to get more Christian billionaires.

Get into this prophetic covenant walk with God so that you might fulfil and establish God's Kingdom before the King (Jesus) comes back. I beseech you to start changing and sending the testimonies of the results. By the grace of God, a more detailed book on God's Covenant Giving is due to be published by this author in the near future.

Please pray that the Lord will grant this author access into the abundance of His revelation and mysteries concerning covenant giving. The Church needs to understand her dynamics and implications at this critical season of wealth transfer. I believe it is going to be a valuable tool in the hands of the Church.

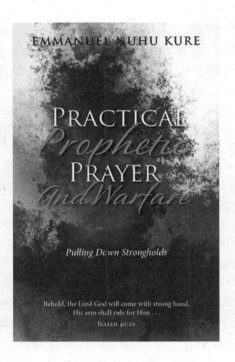

CHAPTER
12

PRACTICAL PROHPETIC PRAYER

The **King's matter** is urgent. God is raising people every-where. He sees willing and able vessels who will network with one another to accomplish specific assignments towards establishing the absolute authority of His Kingdom. That is why it is important to take the commission seriously.

The destinies of nations are in the hands of serious-minded people, not merely religious people. If you are going to play religion, you can continue until Jesus comes back.

When you eventually wake up from your religious slumber, it will be too late, and others will have received the crowns. Until you get into the practicality of Kingdom business, you do not have a portion in our generation. That is what we are called to do - to trample upon anything that stands against us. I am not afraid to die because I have a good story to tell in heaven as my testimony.

There appears to be a generational gap in the Church. As you look around you, you are compelled to ask, "Where are the older men who used to learn battle in those days, those men of old who took their place in the fiercest battle zones of those days?"

They have gone on to retirement. That is why today, God has to raise a new army. He has to recruit people to fill vacancies created by those who have gone on self-exile and spiritual retirement.

There is one thing I never tire talking about. I shall repeat this message over and over. It is the battle cry, my friend. The day of war has come - the day of your emancipation has come. Let the Church get armed. Let's get out and finish once and for all the work entrusted to us. I am eager to go to heaven. I am eager that we wind up on this earth and return to eternal things. But, unfortunately, we can't go until the earthly work is done.

GIVE ME THIS MOUNTAIN

This land we live in is not too big to possess. Caleb came out and said, "Give me this mountain." No matter how many giants reside in the land, we can subdue and possess it. Nothing is impossible; the land can hear us.

There is a priesthood that God is raising in our generation with a different dimension but the same God. By the principles that you learn now, you can set your battle ensigns and declare war, and your spirit will be let loose. With it, your situation will normalize and your nation, too, will be set free.

Everything that makes up a nation has ears to hear. There are demons that have been put in place to rule. But we also have angels in charge. The Lord has placed us in the land that we may rule, take control and dominate the land. If the land under you gets rebellious, you have to bring it under control. There is nothing too hard for you to bring under control. It is because we have chosen to do God's work according to our own ways and imaginations that our wills have been placed above the will of God. *"For lack of knowledge, my people perish."*

No matter how unpleasant our land is, it is never the wish of God for us. People are often the reason for difficult situations.

"And said unto them, Ye are the chief of the fathers of the Levites: sanctify yourselves, both ye and your brethren, that ye may bring up the ark of the Lord God of Israel unto the place that I have prepared for it. For because ye did it not at the first, the Lord our God made a breach upon us, for that we sought him not after the due order" (1 Chronicles 15:12-13).

David was the cause of Uriah's death. If David had done the right things, Uriah would not have died; this much David him-self admitted in 1 Chronicles. The Bible says that if we do not do things according to the heavenly order, we are bound to face unpleasant consequences.

May the Lord teach you the divine pattern. Let it be clear to you that when you walk in His path, your destiny will open up unto you.

The stone has ears. Joshua told the children of Israel they had vowed to serve the Lord and not the gods of their fathers.

"And Joshua said unto all the people, Behold, this stone shall be a witness unto us; for it hath heard all the words of the Lord which he spake unto us: it shall be therefore a witness unto you, lest ye deny your God")Joshua 24:27).

A stone, an inanimate object we ordinarily take for granted, can be a witness for your defense or your destruction.

The bed you lie on bears witness. Likewise, so does the car you ride in. Also, the very biro or pan you use reports you to God every day. When you lie to pastors, the very clothes you wear shall bear witness against you.

Life and the mysteries of God are more complex than a lot of us think. That is why the kingdom of darkness can manipulate lives and tell us that the more we see, the less we understand. Henceforth, your understanding shall be brightened but they (the forces of darkness) shall understand less because God is going to set you loose after which nothing will be able to withstand you. Anything that stands before you, you will trample upon them in Jesus' name.

I have reached a point in my spiritual growth where, if anyone lies when he borrows my car, the car will break down because it bears witness. That is the level of relationship I've established with my property. My staff can testify to this. When they say they are going to the marketplace but attempt to venture beyond the market, the car would not get them to where they want to go. It would break down between the market and their destination. Even when they secretly engage a mechanic to get it going, the car will not respond until it gets to my knowledge. But the moment I appear on the scene, the car would pick up. All it wants to do is report their unfaithfullness.

Oh! that our lives will begin to follow heavenly principles so that we may get heavenly results. We do not get heavenly results because we are busy manipulating rather than operating heavenly principles. When you manipulate, you get human results. God wants to be our help but we put so much of human wisdom into our work that God can only watch in amazement.

God has been my help and I am always happy to announce it everywhere I go. I can give you mind-boggling testimonies to buttress this.

There is a great revival going on. You'd better join the bandwagon of God. Otherwise, you will lose out of it.

All that the earth is waiting for is to get mobilized and today the Lord is going to mobilize you so that you can in turn mobilize the earth. When this is done, there will be riots both in the spiritual and in the physical realms. When the earth is mobilized, it will stand up and say, *"Yes, the Lord reigneth. Blessed be the name of the Lord for the Lord our God He is Omnipotent. He reigneth in majesty."*

Because the stone bore witness in Joshua 24, it became a pattern for the children of Israel to take twelve stones and lay them across for an altar on which they poured oil whenever they crossed a river.

That was why after Jacob had finished dreaming, he poured

oil, made a covenant with God, and prayed. The stone saw when heaven came down. Hence, heaven would not change its mind concerning the covenant.

"And Jacob rose up early in the morning, and took the stone that he had put for his pillows, and set it up for a pillar, and poured oil upon the top of it. And he called the name of that place Bethel: but the name of that city was called Luz at the first. And Jacob vowed a vow, saying, If God will be with me, and will keep me in this way that I go, and will give me bread to eat, and raiment to put on, So that I come again to my father's house in peace; then shall the Lord be my God: And this stone, which I have set for a pillar, shall be God's house: and of all that thou shalt give me I will surely give the tenth unto thee" (Genesis 28:18-22).

From the beginning of the earth, the earth was programmed to sustain and protect man. The soil you walk on has been oriented to keep you alive. Part of its codes of conduct is to keep you alive and to protect you. Any day it disagrees with you or takes your life, it becomes rebellious. The Bible says:

"And surely your blood of your lives will I require; at the hand of every beast will I require it, and at the hand of man; at the hand of every man's brother will I require the life of man" (Genesis 9:5).

I am here passing on to you those principles I've learned in my several years through life and death situations. You can imagine a situation where Muslims gathered together in Kano and said, "We will kill this man overnight." Twelve of us were listed for execution with my name at the head of the list because I was like an inspiration to many in that area.

The Lord came in on the night before they could do anything

and gave to their leader a revelation of a fountain of blood, telling them:

"This is the blood of those you want to destroy. But I tell you, except you remove your hand from the blood, this blood you see shall never leave you."

But the man could not understand what this meant. As he woke up in the morning and set to take his breakfast, his tea became blood as it touched his mouth. In the afternoon, when he went to take rice, the scooped rice became a spoonful of blood. For the first time in his life he had to fast for twenty-four hours. He had never done that in his entire lifetime. By nightfall, he was already dying ot hunger. At last he was forced to say, "This surely must be God's judgment."

We have on several occasions similarly seen the finger of the Lord as a sign of His mercies and the physical intervention of the Holy Spirit so that, rather than hearing testimonies, we ourselves became testimonies. Like John said:

"That which was from the beginning, which we have heard, which we have seen with our eyes, which we have looked upon, and our hands have handled, of the Word of life; (For the life was manifested, and we have seen it, and bear witness, and shew unto you that eternal life, which was with the Father, and was manifested unto us)" (1 John 1:1-2).

I am a testimony of God's finger that Jesus is alive. God is doing a new thing. You either join Him or risk being left behind. Do not be like Elisha's generation who, though they knew a double anointing was going to fall, allowed only Elisha to get it. This made them onlookers till the end. May God never allow you to be an onlooker till the end as it means you will not have all the fullness of the Godhead.

Therefore, the next time you see a snake sent by a herbalist to threaten you in the dream, look at it straight in the eye and say, "Thou rebellious animal, you rebelled in the beginning and you were dealt with. And behold, the spirit of rebellion has not left you. The Lord rebukes you. It is written that the seed of the woman shall bruise your head."

Before you curse the spirit behind the serpent, curse the serpent first, then curse the spirit behind it because the serpent owes you allegiance. You are a king while he is your subject. Each time a snake is sent against you, it is being rebellious and since you are the ruler, send your word against it. Release fire upon it, and the herbalist will not send a snake against you again.

The next time you hear a bird chirping by your window, open your window and tell it, "You rebellious animal, the Lord rebuke you in Jesus' name. By the authority of God vested in me, by the spiritual law that rules the earth, by the finger of the Lord Jesus and the covenant I have in Him,

I pull down His finger against your head. I destroy your existence on earth. You are not fit to live. In the name of Jesus I command that you do not die here - carry your message of death back to your sender and release the affliction you brought to me against him."

it is time to get violent. Only violent Christians will survive these perilous times. It is time to receive a fire - only the fire of God will come alive. If you are the lazy Christian who does things sluggishly, you may die before your time. It is high time we learn these principles. it is by them we live and have our whole being.

It is high time the Church woke up from her slumber. It is

high time we stopped being unrealistic, presumptuous people and start being the practical, forward-looking people that we ought to be. It is time to stop having good revivals or good meetings alone. It is time for you to become that revival in the bush, the revival in the land, the revival on the street and the revival in your nation.

It is time for you to become the instigator - the opener of the earth, the one that makes the earth give back its wealth to men. It is time to throw away those constricting things and begin to exist as God exists on high:

"Thus saith the LORD, which giveth the sun for a light by day, and the ordinances of the moon and of the stars for a light by night, which divideth the sea when the waves thereof roar; The LORD of hosts is his name: If those ordinances depart from before me, saith the LORD, then the seed of Israel also shall cease from being a nation before me for ever" (Jeremiah 31:35-36).

The sun can hear you. This is the mystery of how to control the earth, affect it and possess the land. Religious things cannot help us possess the land. If the land is not broken, you cannot take it over. Satan would only keep dribbling it out to you.

You can cease to be a nation before God forever if those ordinances that bind the heaven and the earth cease to stand before the Lord. If those ordinances that control animals cease to stand before the Lord, they can rebel and trample upon us. When this happens, the earth will begin to open up and eat up all our crops and destroy our children. The climate too, will descend upon us with all kinds of sicknesses and diseases.

TOUCH NOT THE ANOINTED
There are heavenly provisions made available to the Church

by God to enable man to rule the earth. That is why the Bible says:

"When I consider thy heavens, the work of thy fingers, the moon and the stars, which thou hast ordained; What is man, that thou art mindful of him? and the son of man, that thou visitest him? For thou hast made him a little lower than the angels, and hast crowned him with glory and honour. Thou madest him to have dominion over the works of thy hands; thou hast put all things under his feet" (Psalm 8:3-6).

If there were no laws subjecting nature unto you, it would trample upon you day and night. After God made a law giving you dominion over the earth, He made a second law making it subject to you. Therefore, there are two decrees standing in this matter: one that makes you a ruler and the other that subjects the earth to you.

Whoever breaks this law is liable to judgment and consequent punishment. If you break it and allow nature to control you, you are liable to judgment. That is exactly what is happening now. Because we have allowed nature to control us, we are frightened by natural things, even small rats that should be scared by our mere presence!

The Church is increasingly defensive. Yet we go to church dressed in our best and singing "Hallelujah, Jesus conquered the world." How can He be said to have conquered the world in your life when you live in fear day and night?

You make Christ to be ashamed of you every time you cringe in fear at the sight of creeping objects. Child of God, where is your authority? Where is your dominion? Where is your rulership? Why don't you say, "O, thou that maketh noise in my sleep, shut up and let me sleep in the name of Jesus!" And because that thing can hear you, it has to obey you.

The Bible says everything that God created, He did by the word of His power. Hence, they understand and obey the authority of the word. When you speak, your own word, they will not obey you. But, when you speak the word of God to them, everything will bow to you.

That was why the donkey could open its mouth and speak to the foolish prophet Balaam who thought he knew everything. The animal said, "My friend, stop beating me. Don't you know that I am trying to save your life?" For the first time a donkey spoke. It means it had been hearing all along just like other animals. They are also able to hear and speak either to be the source of your protection or your destruction.

When ten armed robbers attacked my house in 1996, the word of God stood against them. They could not break through because the finger of God was there with me. I have a covenant binding God. It is the fence surrounding my house and me. It is scriptural. By that covenant, my fence relates with me. The Bible says:

"And in that day will I make a covenant for them with the beasts of the field, and with the fowls of heaven, and with the creeping things of the ground: and I will break the bow and the sword and the battle out of the earth, and will make them to lie down safely" (Hosea 2:18).

God said, *"I will make..."* This means you can ask God to make things happen for you and everything around you to begin to obey your voice. This is the key to possessing the land. With this authority, we can stop any government from making obnoxious laws, except the ones that come from heaven.

My knowledge of the mystery has kept our ministry and us

from begging for bread. When you are a minister who speaks the word of God according to the will of God - that is without superimposing your own will - you will survive every system because you will be supported by people who appreciate what you do in their lives and in the life of the nation.

You should now understand why Moses said, *"Who is on the Lord's side, come forth."* Now, in that scripture, did Moses command the earth to open up and swallow the others people? The earth knew the other people were evil and should be destroyed. Therefore, the earth declared a demonstration and immediately there was an earthquake. When this happens, it means natural things are on your side. An earthquake will not kill your child. It will not demolish your house. Instead, it will crumble the houses of all your enemies.

The Bible says that after every person on the other side had been swallowed up, Moses was still standing tall. The binding was by Moses' speech. When the earth finished its job, it closed up and Moses was free. The earth will protest any day if one hair of my head falls off (Numbers 16).

"For I will take away the names of Baalim out of her mouth, and they shall no more be remembered by their name. And in that day will I make a covenant for them with the beasts of the field, and with the fowls of heaven, and with the creeping things of the ground: and I will break the bow and the sword and the battle out of the earth, and will make them to lie down safely. And I will betroth thee unto me for ever; yea, I will betroth thee unto me in righteousness, and in judgment, and in lovingkindness, and in mercies" (Hosea 2:17-19).

The Bible says from the heavens it shall be spoken *"It is cancelled: that name can no longer work on this man's life."* This is because there is a covenant between the God of heaven, your property and you. This is no mysticism. It is the Scripture revealing to us why we still exist and can walk freely all over Nigeria now.

Four days before General Babangida resigned or "stepped aside," policemen were sent to arrest me in a Full Gospel Business Men's Fellowship program at Mushin Century Hotels. An assistant commissioner of police led the team. They said they had heard that there was a troublemaker at the program from the north. But the Full Gospel executives said, "Sorry sir, you can't arrest our speaker."

They had obviously mistaken me for a National Democratic Coalition (NADECO) spokesman because I dared to preach the truth as revealed from heaven concerning Nigeria. Convinced that I was not a NADECO representative, the search team left. As a priest, my path had never crossed that of the NADECO people and neither did I look like Beko. I thank God He intervened and saved me from the clutches of the police.

After the program, I travelled to Minna to await the return of General Babangida because I was part of the welcoming party for him. Many Christians do not know the details of the mystery of how General Babangida relinquished power. What they thought was that the prayer they offered three months earlier had just come to pass, not knowing that throughout the three months, God lined up watchmen who moved and talked each day by their sacrifices. God picked them from all over the nation.

We raised an altar before the Lord in Minna and made the land to call him back home. Every day of the month, somebody made a sacrifice in the name of the Lord according to divine orders and patterns. This made every sorcery and enchantment they did to keep Babangida in power fail because we were there to ensure that he returned home.

Just as we counted the days of General Babangida, so did we count the days of General Abacha. As surely as the Lord lives, every prophecy that came through us, as revealed by heaven concerning General Abacha, was fulfilled.

The storm or the thunder can hear. When the herbalist turns them against you, you can turn them against the herbalist himself. It is this same principle that the herbalists use against us. They pick a portion of the Scripture, the order they know in the heavenly places, abuse and insult it until the spirit and mystery that holds it gets angry and begins to send out arrows in anger. They then pick up the arrows and send them back to the saints whom those things are supposed to protect.

All the saints often do is respond by pleading the blood of Jesus and hiding under their beds or running after men of God to pray for them, asking prophets to prophesy to stop the storm. Of course, a prophet can stop the storm. But it will continue to pursue you because you have not learned to say, "O, be still" whereupon it will calm down before you. This is what the earth is waiting for now - for the true masters, the true rulers to take control of affairs.

"For the earnest expectation of the creature waiteth for the manifestation of the sons of God. For the creature was made subject to vanity, not willingly, but by reason of him who hath subjected the same in hope, Because the creature itself also shall be delivered from the bondage of corruption into the glorious liberty of the children of God. For we know that the whole creation groaneth and travaileth in pain together until now" (Romans 8:19-22).

I once preached in one of the biggest, most sensitive and powerfully active Anglican churches in Zaria. When I say powerful, I mean financially very rich. The key members were largely occultists who had been traditional church members for many years. Some of them had, indeed, reached the seventh order in the occult world. We started talking about altars and then went into the mysteries of how the planets operate and how the world operates according to the Scripture. I spoke about how the devil abuses the planets, and the attendant results of that abuse.

By the time I finished, three of the church members heading three of the different occult sects in Zaria came out by themselves to give their lives to Jesus. Once the leaders surrencered to Christ Jesus, the junior ones naturally came out to join their masters to serve the true Savior, Master and Lord -- Jesus Christ.

They told me a mystery later. One of them called me outside and said, "Kure, we were fooled that only we had his monopoly of knowledge. We were told that Satan is the originator of power. It was the most senior master in the spiritual realm, the astral realm, who taught us these things. We were told all kinds of things and we went under invocation and, truly, those things worked."

They marveled at how I learned all those things I had spoken about since every detail I gave of how they operated was correct. I told them the Lord Jesus Christ alone taught me. It was then that they realized that the real source of power, the real source of life, exists by the command of the Lord. I told them that it was because the priests had followed their own will that they lost the power, and they had obviously not discovered the mystery hidden inside the Scripture.

Many Christians are too concerned about mundane things like food, what they will put on, etc. They, to their detriment, care less about the main issue that controls the mundane. As a result, they miss the real thing (the Spiritual), which is the bedrock of life.

Yet these are the same Christians who gave their lives to Christ so that they could begin to live according to the will of the Lord! If you belong to this category, certainly the Lord Who is the Perfecter of these things can chisel away the imperfection in your life and in those principles by which your lived before, if you are ready to allow the perfect God, the God of heaven, to Lord Jesus Christ, to take His place in your life. It is then you will understand why He said:

"And into whatsoever city or town ye shall enter, enquire who in it is worthy; and there abide till ye go thence. And when ye come into an house, salute it. And if the house be worthy, let your peace come upon it: but if it be not worthy, let your peace return to you. And whosoever shall not receive you, nor hear your words, when ye depart out of that house or city, shake off the dust of your feet" (Matthew 10:11-14).

The fact that the dust can be a witness means it has a mouth to speak and is powerful enough to deal with any situation. You can take up dust and prophesy against every wicked thing upon the altars by saying, "As they use this sand against me, it shall not prosper," and it shall be so. If a herbalist picks up a leaf, bites it and pronounces a curse upon you, you can reverse it.

Leaves are supposed to give your life. But when someone takes them and causes them to get rebellious against you, you can stop this by prophesying to the leaf to never again rebel against you.

For every blood spilled on the ground, the ground sends forth a curse. This is why the devil rejoices whenever blood is spilled on the ground.

"And the Lord said unto Cain, Where is Abel thy brother? And he said, I know not: Am I my brother's keeper? And he said, What hast thou done? the voice of thy brother's blood crieth unto me from the ground. And now art thou cursed from the earth, which hath opened her mouth to receive thy brother's blood from thy hand" (Genesis 4:9-11).

Note the personification there: *"... **opened her mouth to swallow thy brother's blood...**"* This means the earth has feelings. It can taste and it knows what is right and what is wrong. It is by the word of the Lord that the earth submits to you to be trod upon. Otherwise, it can open up and swallow you down into its bowels filled with water because the Bible says, "The whole earth was full of water." An awareness of the ability of the earth to swallow is what the herbalists use against their victims.

Some children of God still ignorantly go to herbalists and sorcerers to put protective charms on their cars, etc., so that things can be well with them, when in fact, they have anointing oil and the sword of the Spirit in their mouth! When you release your anointing oil and the sword, you too become a medicine man immediately.

With these weapons, you can change your destiny for the better. At this juncture, let me make this clear: Please, it is not the anointing oil that changes the situation. Rather, it is your understanding and application of the ordinances of the heavens that dominate the circumstances on earth as revealed by the word of God. This is to avoid the possibility of defying the anointing oil and going into error.

"Knowest thou the ordinances of the heavens? Canst thou establish the dominion thereof in the earth?" (Job 38:33 ASV).

It as reported in a daily newspaper that, at the sight of blood flowing at an accident scene, demons were walking upon dead bodies laughing hysterically. Blood releases demons as they release curses according to the pattern of Genesis 4:9-11. Demons carry the curse and channel them to particular places they want to take over.

You are the only one who can stop them and their herbalist agents before they take over. This explains why Satan instigates people to shed blood at every possible instance to advance his ministry of killing, stealing and destroying man and his environment. But I thank God that Jesus came that we might live and live well.

Each time Elisha sent his prophets to carry out a prophetic action, it was to turn around natural situations. When he sent one of the sons of the prophets in 2 Kings 9 to go and anoint Jehu as king with the oil as a contact point, Elisha was drawing the judgment of the Lord against Ahab.

The anointing for this was already hanging in the air because it was a judgment God had passed before that time, only that the hour of fulfillment had come and somebody had to be instrumental to its fulfillment.

When the hour of fulfillment comes, except you come down to make contact with the place where it is supposed to be fulfilled, it will hang in the air and will never be fulfilled. If you do not understand this principle, you had better understand it today. This was why, in the days of Jeremiah, after Daniel had read the book and discovered that the years were complete, he began to seek the face of the Lord that the oil might be released to bring about the physical manifestation of that thing.

This was a day of fulfillment which Daniel brought down through prophetic action. That is why, these days, people must go to the place of war, make contact with it and say, "Thus says the Lord, This be the day of my visitation, and by the word of the Lord, I command you to give me my portion. I curse the curses that came out from you against me, and I destroy the altars. I destroy every covenant that is contrary to my life that makes war against my spirit.

"I rebuke every physical or natural thing that is on your side. I command you to give way. Whether they are beasts of the forest, things that creep on the ground, the things in the city or the things in the air, let them give way. By this anointing, I place a demand on you to do righteousness unto me."

Then as you place that oil, and because the words you have spoken are spirit, they go into the very fabric of that thing and begin to release it to do you the righteousness and favor which some demons had stopped before. By that prophetic action, you have reopened it to do you righteousness.

Elisha had to do that for judgment to come upon Ahab. With the touch of that oil he was bringing the hand of that prophecy from Ahab upon Jehu and giving him enough ability to destroy Ahab.

Do you know that Jehu destroyed Ahab by the anointing of God, by the finger of God? It was because he had schemed his order to become king. When you begin to take the things around you by that kind of violence, things will change.

That was why Jesus told them not to stay in their houses and pray for them to get born again. Of course, you can get the power while staying in your house. But you need to take one more step outside. Arise, go to them. When you go to them, you can change your destiny.

By the very composition of man, everything around him was made for him to possess. By the very composition of your priesthood, everything from head to toe is meant to be possessed. The Bible says even the hairs of your head are counted. God has a covenant with the hairs of your head.

"And he that is the high priest among his brethren, upon whose head the anointing oil was poured, and that is consecrated to put on the garments, shall not uncover his head, nor rend his clothes; Neither shall he go in to any dead body, nor defile himself for his father, or for his mother; Neither shall he go out of the sanctuary, nor profane the sanctuary of his God; for the crown of the anointing oil of his God is upon him: I am the Lord" (Leviticus 21:10-12).

Zechariah 4 tells us about the end-time Church. The Bible says there was golden oil going through the golden pipe directly from the Lord that facilitated the spreading of the power, the anointing and the mystery of the seven spirits of God.

The perfection of the anointing of God is made up of the seven spirits. Those seven spirits flow in the golden oil from on high. Agreeing with Leviticus 21, Zechariah 4 says that there is a bowl on his head into which the oil pours and gathers. It is the oil of the Lord.

Whoever touches it will die. Only holy things can touch that oil. That is why I often advise people not to release their head to just anybody to hay hands on it. Otherwise, some people will release all kinds of demons into their body. Your head is a major spiritual entrance into your body.

Even if you were never lustful before but because you submitted your head for anointing on every altar and revival you go, or for every minister whose history you do not know, demons may be transferred onto you. That minister who lays hands on you may be a secret agent of hell, or belongs to the lifeline of Jezebel by which he harbors fornication in his life - only that the report has not come out in the open yet. But you can be sure that every time he lays hands on you, he will transfer the demons of lust to you.

If you wish to remain spiritually alive, you had better heed this. Do not allow just any man of God to lay hands on you at will, no matter how important he is. Some of them do it out of competition with one another to show that they have a greater anointing.

The nose carries the breath of God. The Bible says the Spirit of the Lord is in your nostrils.

"As God liveth, who hath taken away my judgment; and the Almighty, who hath vexed my soul; All the while my breath is in me, and the spirit of God is in my nostrils; My lips shall not speak wickedness, nor my tongue utter deceit" (Job 27:2-4).

Through your nose, you can breathe in the life of God. When the life enters, it kicks out every foul thing that is not part of your system. The life of God can set you free. In Port Harcourt, Rivers State, Nigeria, mere breathing healed a lady. People get healed at our conferences just by breathing in and out.

There is an eye of understanding. The anointing goes through the hand, the one that comes from the golden veil. Then there is one which, when the Spirit of God speaks, acts as the eye of your understanding to receive it. This is the eye of revelation.

Many Indians (the Hindus) put a dot on their forehead as the third eye. It is a mystical covenant eye. There is a demon always seated there. However, from the inner revelation, that is the eye of understanding. A child of God can receive a message from God.

In Habakkuk 3, the Bible says that the Lord came from Teman and that from His hands came out horns of fire.

"God came from Teman, and the Holy One from mount Paran. Selah. His glory covered the heavens, and the earth was full of his praise. And his brightness was as the light; he had horns coming out of his hand: and there was the hiding of his power" (Habakkuk 3:3-4).

It is the hand anointing by the Spirit that is stretched forth for warfare, for protection and for occupation. That is why the Bible says, *"Lay no hands suddenly on anyone..."* I am always cautious not to lay hands on people freely. Even after preaching, I do not shake hands carelessly. Likewise, I do not touch people anyhow because that which the Lord put inside finds an outlet - a voice - in the hand.

That is why you can say "Stop! O Kingdom of darkness," and when they see the fires from you hand, they have to stop. That is why the Bible again says, "You shall lay hands on the sick and they shall be well," because virtue issues out from your hands.

My hands and my eyes talk. With my eyes, I can cast out demons. When you come close to me and I breathe into you, your sickness has to disappear. By breathing, I can transfer my covenant to you because the Spirit of the Lord is in my nostrils. Anointing flows through my nostrils and not just through my hands.

Having understood this strategy, when you make a war cry, the hosts of darkness will run because you are taking them out by revelation. That is what makes the difference - by understanding, by knowledge, you are able to trample on the enemy and take the country - to subdue the land.

My leg is capable of cursing and blessing. With it, I can both curse and bless. I decide whom it curses and whom it blesses. When you understand these things, you can tell God to make all of them play their roles. Wherever your feet tread, you are supposed to conquer. The Bible says:

" *Every place that the sole of your foot shall tread upon, that have I given unto you, as I said unto Moses*" (Joshua 1:3).

Your feet have the capability to possess, to take over and to take control. But for as long as you have not allowed your feet to play their priestly role, they will remain powerless.

In Matthew 10, the Lord Jesus instructed His disciples to dust their feet against any house or city that shut their gates against them. This verse has present- day application in the context of what we have been discussing:

"*And whosoever shall not receive you, nor hear your words, when ye depart out of that house or city, shake off the dust of your feet. Verily I say unto you, It shall be more tolerable for the land of Sodom and Gomorrha in the day of judgment, than for that city*" (Matthew 10:14-15).

It is time to begin to wash your feet. You should wash them with tender care and say, "My feet are the weapons of war." Wash them like you clean the blade of a sword, like you clean a gun and prepare it for war. Declare that, " The anointing of the Lord is upon me, even my legs are anointed to do the righteousness of God on earth among the living in Jesus name."

Each time you go to war, you should be conscious of this. Carry yourself through a separation from head to toe and say, "God, let everything that speaketh in the body begin to speak."

As you step out, the earth will relate to you according to the work from every outlet in your body from head to toe. The ground will not swallow you up. If you use this principle, you will become invincible when you go out on prophetic assignments.

You can remove every mystery of darkness when you exercise the mystery of God. Thank God the Bible says that God has given you everything that has to do with life and godliness. When you know how to operate the mystery of God, everything becomes yours. It was because the prophets of old knew all the mysteries that they were able to send their sons to go and physically step into a place to stamp their authority there.

If you have been due for promotion for many years but someone has stalled the promotion, go and greet the man in the office. Tell God to arm you up. Once you finish telling God to arm you, dedicate anointing oil and anoint that man's office. Take the bottle of oil to his gate. That is what the Bible means when it says, *"It shall be strength unto them that take the battle to the gate."*

At this stage, the battle has come to the physical level because your enemies are now physically stepping into your house. If you stay in your house at this point, they may kill you and you cannot blame God for not protecting you because you are supposed to be as bold as a lion.

That is exactly what the apostle Paul did. He had to go to

Jerusalem himself. His last journey to Jerusalem was not an evangelistic one. It is not written that he went on a missionary journey. He went on a prophetic prayer journey by which he was going to seal up Jerusalem unto destiny. Even when they arrested him, he told his captors that he went to offer alms and to pray in the temple.

He was there to exercise authority over the temple, to transfer life and power and say, "The Lord's name shall be glorified in this temple. Israel shall not be taken away from the covenant of Abraham. Israel shall not be stolen. Israel shall not be conquered by the heathen forces that shall come."

I did not ask for this life that I am living today. It wasn't a positive confession that gave it to me. It was divine favor. God took a look at me and said, "Man, I will keep you alive as long as I need a man." That is why I am still alive.

God is looking for men who will change destinies - men whose lives do not mean anything to them as much as do obedience and the fulfillment of the Scripture. Today, go into your house and prophetically tell everything there, "Hear ye the word of the Lord. You are my property. I did not steal you. Anything that is used against me shall not prosper. None of you shall join any conspiracy against my life. Whoever charms you so that your life should fold up, send the curse back to that person in the name of Jesus.

Also, go into your garden and tell your garden, "O garden, hear the word of the Lord. From now on, pass the word to all your kinds through the wind. O wind, carry it along too. Pass the word to all your kinds, that any herbalist who casts curses against me shall have his mouth filled with boils.

When you say this, any herbalist who tries that shall see the finger of God.

Mobilize your environment against everything that is wicked and evil. Take the soil from the ground and say, "O soil, every wicked man that stands upon you shall not escape God's wrath." Take anointing oil and anoint it.

This is not magic. Jacob did it and God did not condemn him. Say to the soil, "O soil, hear the word of the Lord. By this anointing I put the finger of God upon your life. Henceforth, because you understand spiritual matters, any wicked man that is cooked in hell - that goes through the gate - you will send poison into his nose, especially if the wicked man is bringing evil against you, you will raise a warfare against him to make him know that this ground is holy."

I offer my covenant prayer around my house almost every quarter. My neighbors always say, "I fear that pastor. His own property is different. He walks around the gate!" If you have a fenced gate, go there and speak in tongues round it. All your unbelieving neighbors will begin to fear you from that day because the Bible says the dread of you shall be upon your enemies. You should take up soil, stand in front of your house in the daytime and call upon God to enact your own covenant upon your gate. In fact, the Bible says, *"Write salvation on your gate."*

Begin to do this by mapping out all the trouble spots in your city. Go there and begin to anoint them with oil and say, "Now that I know the revelation, earth, you must hear me -- you must never resist me or be used against me."

Dedicate every property you own unto the Lord and ask them to resist every contention from the pit of hell against you. Walk the length and breadth of your premises to establish your control. Do this and you will have absolute control over nature and every situation. The Bible says:

"And heal the sick that are therein, and say unto them, The kingdom of God is come nigh unto you" (Luke 10:9).

I am not ashamed of the gospel of Christ, for it is the power of God unto salvation. I will exact it upon my walk. I will exact it upon my house. I will exact it upon everything that belongs to the covenant in my life.

Are You Born Again?

If you are not born again, do so now while you are still holding this book because the next second might be too late. Stop running away from God and surrender your life to Him with tears and a broken spirit.

The Holy Spirit and the angels of God that natural eyes cannot see are here with you right now to actualize the redemptive work of Jesus Christ. The same applies to you if you are a backslider or contemplating backsliding. The devil may never allow a more conducive atmosphere until hell catches up with you after today.

Open your Bible to Romans 10:10 and confess your sin. Then declare your salvation in heaven. Don't leave until God answers clearly in your heart.

Saints - Take Heart!

Let the saints take heart and persevere a little longer for the dawn is at hand. Let the saints rejoice in glory and say along with me on their knees and in worship:
"EVEN SO,
COME QUICKLY,
LORD JESUS!"

Remain in His presence and be fortified and transfigured against that day!

Write To Me

Write to me today with your testimonies as I and other people join hands to pray for you and all that await the second coming of our Lord Jesus Christ.

THE THRONEROOM TRUST
(INCORPORATED)

The Throneroom Trust is a tower of strength for the saints. It is a vision to reach, encourage and give direction to the Church in its most trying time. Like Joseph, we have been told to gather now against a time of famine. We have been commissioned to float a mighty Trust through which the Lord will maintain contact with the Body in Nigeria, in particular, and Africa in general.

It is neither a church nor a fellowship anywhere. However, it will encourage the rise of independent interdenominational prayer meetings that will NOT become ministries or churches but will cause the power of God to permeate and rule the world around them be their prayers, and bring revival to their different churches.

It will liaise with any already existing churches in order to serve as a catalyst in preparing the Bride for her Groom. We have the same call as Joseph to prepare for the HOUR OF WANT and the HOUR OF GLORY that will come upon the church. We are like safeguards for the church.

The Lord will have us as saints who will answer the call to carry out this work to cover the following areas:
1. To serve as watchmen over nations, individuals with peculiar callings, churches to fulfill God's preordained destinies. To also watch over God's word and written prophesies in scriptures until they are fulfilled;
2. To support the Church in Nigeria and Africa in the final mighty revival that God is to release on the whole earth;
3. To produce revelations or receive reprint permits to reproduce relevant revival / end-time based Christian literature that will serve as catalysts in bringing the church to glory

for free distribution to all the nooks and corners of Nigeria, Africa and the world. The Spirit of God says clearly to me that this is going to become the sustaining life wire of many lives in this last hour. This will be the major function of the trust when fully established;

4. To reach out to unreached through literature distribution to fulfill an Apostolic mandate over the nations;

5. To develop a very strong base for a Christ-waiting Church in Nigeria and Africa as was practiced in Acts 4:32-37, and receive from the Body all kinds of material gifts and distribute out to the hurting and needy parts of the Church. We believe that Acts 4:32-37 will be fulfilled in our time before rapture;

6. Establish telephone lines known as "Prayer Throne-Lines" used only for those who need emergency prayer, miracle and counseling;

7. Organize gatherings from place to place as booster stations for the Body as found in Joel 2:1 and Jeremiah 8 and 9, where the Body of Christ will meet together to encourage one another (Malachi 3:16-17), receive testimonies of what God is doing around the globe, and understand God's mind and expectations. We will raise a rest camphouse for the revitalization of saints;

8. Enlist volunteers who will offer their substance, time and lives to keep the Church afloat, either on full time or part time basis;

9. To raise strong and solid-based Christ-focused disciples;

10. To raise cities and places of refuge and rest from the vicissitudes of life in this hour.

If you would like to receive our Brochure or Mission Statement or otherwise correspond with us, please write, phone or email us at:

Throneroom (Trust) Ministry, Inc.
Zion International Prayer and Retreat Camp
Throneroom Close, Off Hospital Road
PO Box 266, Kafanchan, Kaduna State, Nigeria.
Tel. +234-8051817164

1114 Bella Vida Blvd.
Orlando, FL 32828, USA
Tel. +1-850-559-0024

E-mail: ttmvisionpioneeroffice@gmail.com
Website: www.throneroomtrustministry.org

You can also write to us for a Kingdom Covenant Partnership Form today and be a Kingdom Partner with us. Or better still, join us as watchmen over the nations if God has called you to watch with us. We have a prophetic ministry with an apostolic mandate to watch over nations and the coming of the King of kings - Jesus Christ.

Our ministry has four cardinal thrusts:
1   Ministry of the watchmen, spiritual gifting, and offices notwithstanding;
2.   Discipleship;
3.   Hospitality; and,
4.   Missions.

Other Books
By Emmanuel Nuhu Kure

While believing you must have been tremendously challenged by this book, we invite you to obtain greater spiritual nourishment by reading the following books by the same author.

The Apostolic Invasion
Confirms that the earnest manifestation of the sons of God cannot become a reality in this age of sophisticated warfare from the kingdom of darkness if the church remains perpetually ignorant of warfare strategies. This is the fact the author seeks to establish as he opens the eyes of the church to basic strategies for warfare to ensure that the saints live a continuously victorious life.

The Invasion From Hell
Embodied prophesies received by the author on contemporary local and global affairs. Some have come true, some are currently coming true while some are yet to be fulfilled.

There have been books of prophecy with varying degrees of accuracy. But one thing the reader will find astonishing is the exactitude with which the prophecies herein are given and the precision with which more have come true.